Changing the World One Backpack at a Time

Changing the World One Backpack at a Time

THE STORY OF MICAH'S BACKPACK AND COMMUNITY ENGAGEMENT

How six people with five backpacks and one school catalyzed community-wide social and economic impact to become known as the project in town that gets things done.

Jennie Hodge and Nancy Franz

ISBN-13: 9781537372181
ISBN-10: 1537372181
Library of Congress Control Number: 2016914418
CreateSpace Independent Publishing Platform
North Charleston, South Carolina

For our families

Table of Contents

Setting the Stage

The story of Micah's Backpack takes place in Blacksburg, a town of 50,000 located in the Blue Ridge Mountains of Southwest Virginia. Virginia Polytechnic Institute and State University (Virginia Tech), the state's Land-Grant University educates 25,000 students and known for studies in agriculture, engineering, and many other disciplines. This vibrant community hosts a variety of arts, sports, and educational opportunities provided by public, private, and civic entities.

St. Michael Lutheran Church located near Blacksburg High School has 409 baptized members. The church's mission states, "As a community of believers guided by the Holy Spirit, the mission of St. Michael Lutheran Church is to: Care for all God's people in need, Hear of God's love through Word and Sacrament Respond to God's grace with thankful hearts, Invite others into Christ's community, Serve God in our daily lives, and Tell the story of God's love for all." The congregation was founded in 1968 when two Lutheran churches merged and built a new church on the site of the first Lutheran church west of the Alleghany Mountains. The church has been led by Pastor John Wertz, Jr. since 2004. Other staff assist with senior adult ministry, administration, music, and Micah's Backpack.

The principle guiding Micah's Backpack, and the umbrella organization Micah's Caring Initiative, comes from the Old Testament book of the Bible Micah chapter 6, verse 8, "And what does the Lord require of you, but to do justice, and to love kindness, and to walk humbly with your God?" Micah's Caring Initiative began with Micah's Backpack. Jennie Hodge has coordinated Micah's Backpack Program since its inception, first as a volunteer and then as the program grew as paid staff. As the main author of this book, Jennie tells the stories included in her voice to help the reader fully experience this important work. Nancy Franz as one of the original initiators of Micah's Backpack assists Jennie in authoring the Micah's Caring Initiative story.

We decided to write this book for a variety of reasons. The most important to share the Micah's Backpack story with others who may want tips and tools to start a similar program. Secondly, we want to contribute to the growing social justice movement through community development and specifically through food security. Lastly, we also enjoy sharing how a few people with a strong vision, energy, and connections can make dreams come true for individuals, organizations, and the community.

Unless otherwise cited, all quotations in the text come from Jennie's conversations or written communications with the people quoted. In some cases, we omit speakers' names to protect their privacy. We thank the many people who have helped shape this story of Micah's Backpack.

CHAPTER 1
Disrupting Positively

The Positively Disruptive Legacy of Five Backpacks

Each day, we experience disruptions that change our expectations and actions. Some disruptions are negative, while some are positive. Some disruptions help us learn; others test our resolve. Disruptive innovations sometimes help us move to the next level of success or satisfaction. An intentional disruption can change how we learn or behave or can improve social, environmental, and/or economic conditions in our community.

In 1997, Harvard University's Clayton Christensen published research on the role of disruptive innovations in the business world. In his view, a disruptive innovation changes and challenges the status quo by improving the affordability, accessibility, capacity, responsiveness, simplicity, or customization of a process or product. This type of disruption usually conflicts with the current way things are done.

Disruptive innovations directly affect our daily lives. For example, one socially disruptive innovation was the founding of the Girl Scouts of the United States in 1912. At the time, Juliette Gordon Low's idea that young women should thrive out of doors, be physically active, and be publicly engaged as active leaders in their communities was radical. Now this view is a societal norm. More recently, online shopping has changed how we purchase goods and services, cell phones and social media have changed how we communicate, and online free open-source education and other resources have changed how we learn.

Micah's Backpack

One evening in September 2007, six members of St. Michael Lutheran Church in Blacksburg, Virginia, met in the church fellowship hall to discuss a new opportunity to help their community. Pastor John Wertz Jr. had read about backpack feeding programs that provide weekend meals for hungry students and wondered if St. Michael should try such a program. They decided to start with five backpacks for low-resource students at one school near the church.

Less than a decade later, the program has grown from those half dozen church members and five backpacks a week to more than seven hundred volunteers, two hundred fifty partner groups, and almost three hundred "backpacks" (actually plastic grocery bags) distributed each week at ten elementary, middle, and high schools in Montgomery County, Virginia. Spin-off programs under the umbrella of Micah's Caring Initiative include Micah's Mobile Backpack, Micah's Garden, Micah's Soup for Seniors, and Micah's Closet. Micah's Backpack has become a catalyst for community engagement in Blacksburg. As one resident says, "Micah's Backpack is known as the project in town that gets things done."

The members of the original group embraced Pastor John's story of backpack feeding and devised foundational principles for our work. The group agreed to (1) create a community organization to support and guide the effort, (2) limit the focus to schools in the Blacksburg area, (3) start small, and (4) help empower other groups to start programs to serve their communities. These principles have helped shape the organization and contribute to its support and growth.

Most of us in that first group were surprised to hear about the number of area children who qualified for free meals during the school year. When we started Micah's Backpack, 16.5% of the students at Blacksburg's seven public schools qualified for free or reduced-price meals. Less than five years later, as we began to plan for the launch of Micah's Mobile Backpack, the student population relying on the meals had grown to more than 24%. Because families self-report their income for the free meals program and may not return the forms to the school, these numbers may underreport the true number of food-insecure children in our community.

The group decided to pilot the backpack program with one location, an elementary school where one of the original six people worked. We started by providing backpacks of food for students each Friday to decrease hunger over the weekend, when they lacked access to meals at school. The group also determined who would be responsible for buying food, who would oversee packing and delivering backpacks, and how many backpacks this new ministry could afford to deliver each week based on a budget of ten dollars per bag per week. As the school year progressed, we expanded to eighteen bags, adding children at two more elementary schools.

As the school year drew to a close, we looked ahead to the fall. A Virginia Tech student and regular backpack volunteer urged us to reach out to all five of our community's elementary schools. When school resumed in August, we sent six bags to each of the schools. As a result, we began to see a huge increase in the number of community partners interested in sharing their time, financial resources, and ideas. We live in a very generous community, and individuals and partners have provided enough funding that we have never had to exclude a child from the program.

In 2010, we expanded again by adding Blacksburg Middle and High Schools to the program. Youth volunteer Olivia Hodge recalls,

> In my eighth-grade math class, I remember overhearing a classmate complain that he was very hungry, and his mom hadn't been able to go to the grocery store in a month. We had already started Micah's Backpack, but we were only doing the elementary schools, not the middle or the high schools. I decided that hunger is not only for little kids but also kids in my grade and older. I shared this with volunteers at Micah's Backpack, and I told my guidance counselor about the hungry boy. We then decided to start help feeding kids in Blacksburg Middle School and High School. That way every [hungry] child gets food over the weekend.

We started out feeding a dozen kids at the middle school. Within a year, that number had more than tripled, and we have continued to serve between thirty-five and forty students in fifth through eighth grades.

Currently, we share meals and snacks with approximately 280 children every week. In addition to our seven public schools, we deliver bags to younger children at three low-resource preschools. Our participation numbers change slightly as children move in and out of our school system. Families occasionally stop participating in the program when their economic status improves. We recently met a significant milestone: we've shared 350,000 meals!

The concept of weekend backpack feeding for youth and their families started more than two decades ago with a nurse at a Little Rock, Arkansas, elementary school. She recognized that some students suffering from headaches, nausea, and irritability were not ill but hungry. She contacted her local food pantry, the Rice Depot, and a partnership to alleviate weekend food insecurity was born. Micah's Backpack and hundreds of other organizations have been inspired by this original partnership to alleviate hunger and improve academic achievement.

How we prepare the weekly gift of Micah's Backpack for our children has evolved over the past few years. However, one activity remains central throughout the year—on Thursdays, we pack six meals plus snacks for children. Every bag contains two breakfasts, two lunches, three snacks, and two dinners, plus two juice boxes and two milk boxes. We include individually sized, shelf-stable, and easy-to-prepare foods. Virginia Tech students in the Human Food, Nutrition, and Exercise program evaluate and adjust our menu to make our gift as healthy as possible. For example, based on the students' advice, we have switched to from diced fruit packed in syrup to fruit packed in juice, a healthier option. While backpack program organizations vary from community to community, the common mission of feeding hungry children on the weekend remains the same.

According to Michelle Barton, a frequent Micah's Backpack volunteer,

> I feel like we appreciate Micah's because it's targeting a fundamental need, and right, for children.... This one hits home because food is a basic necessity. Most of us grew up never knowing that programs like this existed because we were blessed with circumstances that didn't make it part of our world. Looking back, I can't imagine how I would have felt or how I would have dealt with these issues at such a young age, and I think that's what keeps us all coming back. We can't imagine it, so we don't want any kid to have to live it.

These efforts are appreciated. According to one teacher, "A few weeks ago a child asked me why I always put food in her bag and I said, 'because you are on the list.' She tilted her head, thought for a moment, then said, 'well thanks.'" Another parent wrote,

> We all enjoyed the food but for my son the feeling that he is contributing in the family was very exciting! Sometimes when I made something from HIS grocery! he asked me: Mom, did you use any of *my* school stuff?. He always had a smile on his face when I picked him up from the school bus with heavy food items. I am sure he was enjoying more from the contribution than only eating them.

And another parent reported,

> Thank you for including our daughter as a participant in Micah's Backpack. We were motivated to sign her up about two years ago because her pediatrician was concerned about her lack of growth over the past year. He was afraid that this might affect her brain development—unless she gained weight. Micah's Backpack helped increase the variety in our daughter's diet and give her the extra treats she needs.

Micah's Backpack feeds so many children because we engage many people, thank them, and try to provide a positive experience for anyone supporting our work. We participate in a relational and mutual exchange of resources that causes positive disruptions individually and across our community.

CHAPTER 2
Branching Out

Spin-Offs: Success from a Bottomless Backpack of Possibilities

The expansion of the Micah's Backpack program into Micah's Caring Initiative came from participants' dedication and passion. Volunteers and other supporters have a variety of reasons for participating and deepening their commitment to the work: they want to make a difference for hungry children; they feel useful in their community; they are excited about the program's impact; they are passionate about youth development and/or community development; they have compassion for low-resource families. We also know the Micah's experience sticks with people and garners expanded support. The message is simple (make a difference for hungry youth), the results are unexpected (working on this together makes all of us better), the outcomes are concrete, the program has credibility, the effort is tied to our emotions, and the stories about the program give it staying power. In fact, the efforts keep expanding as more resources and partners join.

The combination of the right purpose, the right people, the right time, and the right methods led to what is sometimes called a tipping point, where the development of related programs flowed naturally from Micah's Backpack. All of the spin-off programs share the mission of supporting low-resource individuals, and we have created the *Micah's brand* to help ensure that all of these efforts consistently reflect our principles:

1. provide an opportunity for people do things they would not usually do
2. build community around a helping project
3. create new partnerships to reach a goal
4. create common space to build community
5. allow project participation in a variety of ways at a variety of times

6. make decisions with low-resource individuals in mind and in collaborative ways
7. use technology to support storytelling, efficiency, and effectiveness
8. show gratitude in relationships, finances, structures, leadership, fellowship, and faith
9. encourage innovation to be as effective as possible

Volunteers and other resources often stretch across several projects to reach more people more effectively. The programs that make up Micah's Caring Initiative provide numerous ways for people to contribute to individual and community betterment.

Micah's Garden

Since we've just unloaded carts of extra food and the cooler from Micah's Mobile Backpack six hours after boarding the bus, I am worn out. This dwindling summer day begins to feel like the drip of water that leaks from the cooler: small and never-ending. I've been on the go, greeting kids and their families, for hours. At some point earlier in the season, scheduling the Potato Party after summer food deliveries seemed like a good idea. Now, not so much. Sticky with sweat and with my hair plastered to my neck and face, I drag myself toward Micah's Garden.

As the sun begins its shimmering descent in the west, I enter the Garden. I am thankful that the gate gives easily when I unlock it, though it is out of balance and hangs slightly askew. As I cross from crunchy grass to mulched pathway, I begin to feel different, a little less tired.

Last year, I remember, I enjoyed digging in the crumbly dirt for potatoes. To me, searching for potatoes in the mounds is a lot like hunting for buried treasure. Soon, I find it easier to be joyful. I greet the long hills, and if I didn't know there were potatoes in them, I'd wonder where we were digging tonight. These plots have transformed themselves in recent weeks. The lush, leafy greenery that grew up toward the sustaining sun has wilted away. In some spots, the mounds look barren, but I know what's inside. We just have to start moving some earth.

Our lead volunteers are working up a sweat that matches mine. They're dressed for the job—worn jeans and boots that have seen better days, work gloves. They lean forward, swiping pitchforks through the dirt and unearthing caches of food for our neighbors.

A dozen of us of all ages watch and wait. Some of us are avid gardeners; others are just pitching in for the evening. Once the folks with the pitchforks have sifted through a section fairly completely, the rest of us get down on our knees among the clods of earth and collect the potatoes by hand. Or at least most of us do. Two preschool aged sisters and a toddler boy have retrieved a faded plastic big digger from the Kids' Dump Truck Garden bed. They load a half dozen or so potatoes into the truck bed and maneuver the vehicle through the potato valleys to the bags where we're collecting our Yukon golds. Then they find their way back for another load.

By the time we finish harvesting, everyone is smiling, marveling at our bounty. Grand total: 185 pounds! Our hands seem not quite so muddy, and our backs seem to ache a bit less. We begin to make ambitious plans for next year: more rows, different potato varieties, and a total poundage guessing game with a prize. We had fun finding the potatoes; better still, they will be welcomed at the food pantry on Friday and will then go on to feed our neighbors. We've done something beautiful while building a stronger, healthier community.

I am grateful to end my day with a double dose of that kind of tired. I am thrilled that so many folks helped in the garden. I am inspired by what happens when each volunteer does his or her part: all of these small voices combine into a wonderful symphony. We have made a huge impact for the food pantry clients. I am especially happy about the young kids who join in the work.

One spring, Pastor John and I discussed transforming some of the grassy area behind St. Michael Lutheran Church into a cooperative community garden. He then sold church leaders on the idea. He recalls,

> Enlisting the support of the Congregational Council for Micah's Garden was much easier because of the success of Micah's Backpack. The momentum and positive energy from Micah's Backpack helped the Council to know that a community-based ministry could succeed. Having funding from grants and individual donors to cover the start-up costs removed any financial roadblocks, and having a clear vision for what Micah's Garden could accomplish made the decision relatively easy, particularly when I promised we would plant grass again if the project failed.

Discussions with potential volunteers and partners helped us refine the concept of the garden, and then the real work began. I requested and received grants to help cover the cost of the largest piece of infrastructure we would need—the fence. Keeping out deer, groundhogs, and other critters would be essential to our effort to share as much food as possible with our human community.

One volunteer researched fences. Based on the information she gathered, we decided we needed a barrier that measured eight feet above ground and extended two feet below the surface to prevent moles, groundhogs, and other varmints from tunneling their way in. A large gate in the middle would permit access on foot and to vehicles when needed. Another volunteer offered earth-moving equipment to help with the installation. Then members of Virginia Tech's Corps of Cadets and two dozen other community residents gathered to erect the fence. Once that was finished, a group from St. Michael, Men in Mission, spent a Saturday in fellowship, building raised beds. The local Virginia Cooperative Extension office gave us seed packets to get started.

After watching us work and venturing over to see what we were doing, the dairy and cattle farmer from across the way generously offered a spare cistern, saving the Garden nearly a thousand dollars. A member of St. Michael adept at carpentry designed a platform to elevate the cistern. An anonymous benefactor purchased a pump that enabled us to get water from the adjacent retention pond to the cistern and in turn to the Garden.

So we had our physical facilities. But how would Micah's Garden operate? Pastor John and I had conceived a traditional, familiar community garden where individual gardeners rent a plot and grow food for themselves, but through our discussions, the plan transformed into a cooperative enterprise. In our model, gardeners might grow produce in any combination: for themselves, to share, or for themselves and to share. In the three years we've been growing food nearly all the gardeners share something from their personal plots.

Micah's Garden is divided into two separate though connected areas. There are twenty-four raised beds, each measuring four feet by eight feet, as well as two larger rectangular plots where raised-bed gardeners and volunteers grow food to share with four food pantries. Individuals rent the smaller beds for thirty dollars per year plus two hours of service to the Garden each month during the growing season. Service comes in many forms—planting, harvesting, delivering to food pantries, weeding the pathways in the Garden.

Micah's Garden and all the other Micah's Caring Initiative programs imitate Micah's Backpack by taking advantage of the skill sets possessed by volunteers (both those who have individual plots and those who do not) and partner groups. We encourage volunteers to use their abilities and time as they choose. Some volunteers prefer to weigh and deliver the produce, whereas others enjoy getting their hands dirty working in the earth. One tech-savvy volunteer monitors the Garden and determines what needs to be done each week. She makes and distributes harvest maps that illustrate each week's tasks. Another volunteer hosts informal social gatherings that enable individual gardeners to get to know one another. The pump is maintained by a volunteer who enjoys tinkering with small engines and who fills and empties the cistern as needed. Volunteers who possess graphic design talents create visual materials to help tell the story of our outreach. Volunteers interested in nutrition and cooking collaborate with a Virginia Cooperative Extension employee to create simple recipes for recipients of the produce. According to Tullio O'Reilly, the supervisor of the Spiritual Roots food pantry, "I have used the recipes as examples and the Virginia Tech Community Nutrition classmates to create even more." The first summer, we shared food at three pantries; after Micah's Mobile Backpack began in 2013, we expanded to include that outreach as well.

In our first growing season, we engaged nearly one hundred volunteers who gave a total of 830 hours of service. The following year, those numbers grew to 125 individuals and 975 hours. Nearly thirty different collegiate organizations, civic clubs, and interfaith groups volunteered at Micah's Garden during its first three years in existence.

Both the amount and variety of the fruits and vegetables shared by Micah's Garden have also increased each year. Production increased from 1,305 pounds of fresh, organic fruits and vegetables the first year to 1,607 pounds the following year. Most of it was grown in the Garden behind the church, although some produce comes from individual donations. As Pastor John explains, "We envisioned producing food and sharing it with food banks locally. It never occurred to me that setting up the distribution system would also create a way [for] people in the community and congregation to donate extra food they were growing in their own gardens."

In response to a suggestion from volunteers, one year between growing seasons, we added a greenhouse, enabling growers to nurture seedlings more efficiently and effectively. Lynn Brammer, a member of the Cooperative Extension Master Gardeners of the New River Valley who helped fund the project, says, "Ongoing awareness of the ever higher numbers that need healthy local options made [us] determined to make a difference. We are proud to be a part of making [Micah's Garden] a continued success." We remain on the lookout for ways to further expand and improve the program as well as for sources of funding to enable us to do so.

Although Micah's Garden is distinct from Micah's Backpack, both programs fall under the Micah's Caring Initiative umbrella, and the Garden uses the same methods that have worked so well in Micah's Backpack: encouraging the community to help, recognizing the distinctive talents volunteers possess, and being grateful for whatever help folks are willing or able to provide, no matter how minor it might seem.

The idea for Micah's Garden arose in part out of a desire to shorten the distance between me and the families who receive food through Micah's Backpack. After all, they are my neighbors and potentially my friends. The work I do with Micah's Backpack during the academic year is at an arm's length. Yes, I feed kids. And yes, the program makes my community better. But I have no direct connection to the families for whom I work.

Little did we know when the idea began to germinate that we really had an ideal situation: volunteers who wanted to help grow food, former farmland that had lain fallow for years, a nearby source of free water, and funders and donors who wanted to support an alternative source for growing and sharing food.

This outreach program has received positive responses from all segments of our community. Volunteer and grower Harold Trease says, "Being able to help make a community garden productive is good for the community, is good for the environment, and keeps a person engaged. There is always a certain amount of satisfaction derived from getting things to grow and produce, but helping make the garden productive enough to help other people is even better." According to Daniel Ferrell, coordinator for a postsecondary school group,

> I took my students/staff (young adults with disabilities) with me this summer on several occasions and then I took my sons one day for an all day garden maintenance day. Helping them to understand what giving back is about and modeling for them and allowing them the opportunity to participate in the giving side of volunteerism and charity is a great feeling, personally, and I was there doing it as well.

Food pantries often distribute grocery store leftovers and shelf-stable, processed foods, so fresh fruits and vegetables are an important and welcome addition to their inventories. According to Brad Grems, a food pantry volunteer,

> We ... have a fairly good understanding of the role of charitable food donations to those with food insecurity. Micah's Garden provides a healthier alternative to processed food. That is the main appeal to us. We really regret that there are not more and larger programs like Micah's Garden that could replace processed high sugar/high carbohydrate foods commonly available to low-income families.

One parent who visited the Mobile Backpack one summer told me, "Our family loves fresh vegetable[s] and fruit[s] and we don't use much canned foods. So we all enjoyed the fresh products." Giving Tree food pantry supervisor Bayley Alphin concurs:

> We are so very grateful for the summer months, when our pitiful supply of fresh produce is ramped up by local gardens, especially Micah's Garden. Each week, volunteers show up with that week's harvest. We go from not having enough produce to pulling out extra tables to keep up with all the fruit and vegetable donations. Our patrons take the fresh donations with enthusiasm, grateful for the healthy and tasty additions to their dinner tables. Many times I have witnessed patrons happily sharing recipes of what they are going to make with the fresh ingredients as they pick through the supply. It is a joy to see all that hard work going to the mouths and bodies of our neighbors who need nutrients the most!

All of these efforts involve community members working together to make it possible for Micah's Garden to share fresh, organic food. Grems sums up our approach:

"Community service, then, is not giving the poor your surplus, but giving them what they really need, which in many cases are not the same thing. Micah's Garden is probably targeted to the real needs better than many other charitable programs."

Micah's Mobile Backpack

On a humid afternoon in late July, a converted school bus lumbered up the repeatedly patched pavement of a local mobile home park. By now, kids and their families had grown accustomed to seeing this particular school bus during the summer. As the bus lurched toward its first stop, the volunteer driver's grin spread as he recognized the kids who lived in a cluster of three mobile homes there.

Brakes on and engine off, the driver climbed down the bus steps and chocked the wheels. When not driving, he served as a lookout of sorts, keeping his eyes open for kids we hadn't met before. The driver and a parent struck up a conversation about Virginia Tech's football prospects for the fall season. Two high-school-aged volunteers grabbed their clipboards and disembarked to greet the waiting kids.

One exuberant boy couldn't hold back his glee: it was Friday afternoon, and the food and books had arrived. He blew past the high-schoolers and charged onto the bus with a huge smile. An octogenarian volunteer smiled back and greeted him by name. She didn't let him slip past her to the books until he filled out his menu for the next week. He knew the routine and gave in. For his main dishes, he checked three cans of tuna and a jar of peanut butter. Next, he chose two fruit cups and skipped the mixed-veggie option. Finally, for snacks, he selected a granola bar and fruit chews. And, like every week, he scribbled "popsicles" in the space set aside for favorite foods. The volunteer chatted with him as he filled out his menu—the two had developed a rapport that erased the seven-decade difference in their ages. When he finished, she announced that she planned to share popsicles on the last day of distribution in late August.

Next, he headed to the back of the bus. The week's book volunteers, two teachers from his elementary school, greeted him warmly and watched as he produced his most recent titles from his bag. He needed no further instructions and chose two new books for the coming week. The teachers recorded his selections, gave him encouragement on his summer reading, and waved good-bye as he headed toward the front of the bus. Three younger kids had finished filling out their menus and jumped on the bus to exchange books.

During all the hustle and bustle, I was waiting on the street at the back of the bus, swigging from a water bottle. As the kids hopped off the final step of the bus, I called to them and hunted through the bins for their food bags. We met and I handed them their personalized weekend food bags. The previous Friday's menu was stapled to each bag, and the kids got whatever they chose, plus the items we always included: two boxes of juice and two of milk.

In addition, this week we shared carrots, tomatoes, blueberries, and corn. Volunteers had planted, grown, and harvested the carrots and tomatoes in Micah's Garden. Another volunteer shared blueberries she selected at the neighboring U-pick farm. The six dozen ears of corn were a gift from local family farmers. The first boy's mother smiled and said that her son would eat the veggies since they came from the bus.

When the half dozen kids had all made their choices, said their hellos and good-byes, and grabbed baggies full of blueberries, thank-yous from kids and volunteers echoed all around as we prepared to move along. Safety chocks came off the wheels. The teenaged volunteers climbed on board and shared a bench seat. One of them related, "Every child deserves to have enough food to eat, and it makes me feel good to see so many people who are happy to take that step up to help make sure that happens." The teachers reorganized the book bins. The driver peeked over his shoulder and checked the rearview mirror for approaching cars. We pulled out of the drive and moved up the hill to the next stop.

For thirteen weeks in the summer of 2013, Micah's Mobile Backpack shared more than seven hundred meals per week as well as an average of almost thirty pounds of fresh produce every week in July and August, much of it grown in Micah's Garden, the cooperative community garden. In addition to bringing the food, we showed food-insecure kids that their community continues to care for them during the summer. So how exactly did I and these other volunteers, young and young at heart, from a college town in southwestern Virginia find ourselves riding along in a school bus passing out food and books? Micah's Mobile Backpack is a response to the childhood food insecurity we encounter in our community. The bus didn't appear magically or immediately. Our revolutionary approach to summertime weekend food delivery grew out of a dream to make a difference in the lives of our young friends and neighbors by extending our school year backpack feeding program. That summer saw the dream come alive and positively impacted improved the lives of at least 150 children a week.

We had already developed the Micah's Backpack program to help kids during the school year. But we wanted to do more. How could we make sure these children had food during the summer months? The Food Research and Action Center, a national hunger advocacy group, reports,

> Only one in seven of the low-income students who depended on the National School Lunch Program [also known as free and reduced lunch] during the regular 2009–2010 school year had access to summer meals in 2010. The limited reach of the Summer Nutrition Programs meant that for the majority of those children, the end of the school year was the end of the healthy, filling meals on which they counted. It also meant a summer of struggling to avoid going hungry.... The number of low-income children who are receiving free or reduced-price lunch during the regular school year is one excellent indicator of the need for summer food.

To solve this problem, we started dreaming big: if the kids weren't in school to get food, we would bring food to them where they were. In the summer of 2013, we launched Micah's Mobile Backpack that operates as a client-choice food pantry on wheels. It delivers directly to kids at their homes and schools. In creating Micah's Mobile Backpack, we applied and adapted the school year backpack model for summer break. I know of no other program with a youth focus for multi-meal summer feeding deliveries.

Before launching Micah's Mobile Backpack, we tried two other models for summer feeding, with mixed results. Heading into the summer of 2010, we thought we had a good, sustainable plan in place to feed kids during the summer break. The county had traditionally held a summer school session at one elementary school, and many of those who attended were the same low-resource kids served by Micah's Backpack. Thus we planned to extend our school-year program for the six-week summer term, delivering bags to the kids at that elementary school. But in the midst of a fiscal crisis, the county school board eliminated the summer session. With too little time to develop a new plan for summer feeding, we decided our best option was to distribute a list of available food resources to our students, hoping their families would use that food assistance.

The following year, we tried again. We decided to provide a week's supply of staples that families could pick up from our distribution location. Rather than providing individual meals for one child as we do during the school year, these bags held boxes of pasta, jars of pasta sauce, large boxes of cereal or oatmeal, cans of fruit and vegetables, and jars of peanut butter. If we were lucky with our food bank shopping, we could include a box of crackers or cookies. We believed that providing so much food would make the trip to pick it up worthwhile for the families.

We called about twenty families living within a couple miles of the distribution center to remind them about the food pickup. The first week, one family came. Nineteen bags remained untouched. The second week, no families came. Volunteers were puzzled. The third week, we called the participating families again: two came.

We changed tactics. We called the families to ask if we could have their addresses so that volunteers could deliver the food, and all twenty agreed. For the rest of the summer, three volunteers drove food to the participants' homes once a week. The children and their parents expressed their gratitude, and this, our first face-to-face contact with the neighbors we served, made a significant impression on me. I experienced one-to-one feeding and fellowship contact that was missing during the academic year. Although this approach helped a small number of families, it was not scalable or sustainable for our organization. We went back to the drawing board.

In the spring of 2012, our food bank partner, Feeding America Southwest Virginia, asked if we would be interested in participating in the U.S. Department of Agriculture's Summer Food Service Program, which provides a variety of free foods, including turkey-and-cheese and peanut-butter-and-jelly sandwiches, milk boxes, and snacks. This sounded perfect for us. Who doesn't love free food to distribute? And we would be going into our community and building relationships, continuing the process we had started the previous summer. It seemed like a win-win. We eagerly signed up.

We met with a representative from Feeding America's children's program and watched a thirty-minute presentation on the Summer Food Service Program. So far, so good. Again, the free food was a huge benefit. We filled out our paperwork and shared the amazing story of free food far and wide, first with volunteers and later with families.

The initial challenge to our participation in the Summer Food Service Program involved finding good locations to distribute food. The USDA requires that the site be at 50% poverty level according to recent U.S. Census data, a requirement that proved more difficult to meet than we expected. Both the front door of our university's conference center hotel and a nearby cemetery met the poverty-level prerequisite, but a partner church across the street from those spots did not.

We ultimately found two qualifying locations. The first was a mobile home park in the northeastern part of town. We planned to serve lunch there once a week. Since 2006, one of our interfaith partners, Blacksburg United Methodist Church, has maintained a mobile home, Fun143, in the park, and that positive presence created a natural fit for us. Children and their families had an existing relationship based on comfort and trust with the staff and volunteers at Fun143. We served lunch there every Thursday that summer. Our volunteers enjoyed the experience, and the kids got a meal before they began working with tutors, playing, or participating in other planned activities. Each week, twelve to fifteen kids joined us for a meal and conversation with us. The site enabled us to reach a lot of food-insecure kids, in large part because of the infrastructure that Blacksburg United Methodist had already developed and nurtured.

Thinking that mobile home parks were ideal locations to reach our target demographic while still meeting the 50% poverty level requirement, we chose another one on the other side of town as our second site. Every week that summer, at least six eager volunteers showed up to share lunches on Tuesdays and Thursdays at the park's playground. However, on most days, the volunteers outnumbered the kids. Disappointed, we tried to figure out why kids weren't coming to the park for lunch. We posted more flyers and asked the kids who came to share the news of the lunchtime meal with their friends and neighbors.

About midway through the summer, the problems with the playground location became clear. A middle-school-aged girl told us in casual conversation that many parents don't let their children come to the playground because it was a prime location for mischief for older teens. Also, the playground was located at one end of the park, too far from many homes for kids to go without parent supervision. Selecting our location without input from the neighborhood had been a huge mistake.

The Summer Food Service Program presented a few other challenges. For one, kids had to eat the lunches in front of us, a requirement that might have deterred shy children from participating. In addition, we overestimated the number of kids who would participate and ended up with a huge amount of extra food. As a consequence, we had to call our grocery store partner to ask for space in their walk-in freezer to store hundreds of extra sandwiches until we could share them with other hunger relief agencies. Ultimately, as much as the volunteers enjoyed building relationships with the kids we met, the USDA program did not fulfill our ultimate objective. We are a weekend feeding program, and that is our mission. Providing lunches was nice, but it was not our mission.

These two attempts at summer food distribution provided valuable knowledge and experiences, and we began to develop our own unique plan for a summer feeding program. We realized that transportation issues presented one of the biggest hurdles to feeding food insecure kids during the summer. Around 5% of Blacksburg's households do not have vehicles, and many of these families are the same ones whose children we serve during the school year with Micah's Backpack. We needed a way to get the food to them during the summer. We needed to create a mobile backpack program.

Pastor John was completely supportive and provided help and encouragement throughout the process. He knew that a mobile backpack "was a solution that came with many unique issues. Where would we get the money to get started? Should we get a bus or a trailer? How would it really work? We didn't have the answers to any of those questions, but we knew that Micah's Mobile Backpack was where we needed to go." We would expand on the Summer Food Service Program by pinpointing the needs of the youth in our community, demonstrating our community's commitment to them even when school was not in session.

Having learned from our earlier experiences, we solicited input from the parents of the children we served as we entered the planning process. A February 2012 telephone survey of families who received food during the school year found that 92% of the parents indicated that weekend food in the summer would be helpful. Many parents also confirmed our sense that transportation barriers impeded their ability to get food.

Armed with numbers and summer feeding stories, I dove into the grant application process. In April 2012, I submitted a letter of inquiry to the Community Foundation of the New River Valley, which was launching a new Community Impact Grant program. We were invited to move forward with our summer feeding plan, and I spent many hours crafting what I hoped would be the perfect grant proposal: part data and part firsthand anecdote. After we submitted the application, the Community Foundation invited us to its offices to talk about our proposal and answer questions. In August, we learned that we had received a ten-thousand-dollar grant to fund Micah's Mobile Backpack. Many months of dreaming, researching, writing, and crossing fingers had paid off.

The Community Foundation's announcement explained, "Micah's Backpack has had a tremendous impact in Blacksburg and continues to come up with creative ways to provide nutritious meals for children in need. We are so pleased to award our very first Community Impact Grant to Micah's Mobile Backpack."

The idea of mobile food is not unique. However, our concept of mobile food targeting out-of-school kids is novel. Many regional food banks have launched refrigerated mobile pantries that provide staples and perishable foods to partner agencies, typically in rural areas. Feeding America Southwest Virginia, for example, has a mobile pantry that visits very remote areas, but food-insecure children are not its focus. Since we had no model to follow, we devised a program from scratch. We decided that a converted bus would work best. This meant that we needed to find one. We would also need a large number of volunteers as well as the participation of our community garden partners so we could share fresh food. Between September 2012 and June 2013, volunteers, Pastor John, and I drafted, revised, and redrafted plans until we had a workable blueprint for Micah's Mobile Backpack. We settled on two tentative routes that emphasized the higher-poverty neighborhoods, made contacts with our partner locations and mobile home park offices to announce the plan, and recruited volunteers.

As word of our new program spread in our community, volunteers with specialized knowledge and talents began to offer their help. Bryan Katz, a school bus aficionado and traffic engineer, worked his connections and found the perfect bus for a great price. He later recalled, "I was extremely honored to help. I was excited to be able to contribute my talents and knowledge of school buses to identify the bus that would best fit the needs of the program. Having a shorter bus that is easier to drive, with air conditioning, and with a wheelchair lift I felt provided the perfect combination for our program!" Because the bus is wheelchair-accessible, it has no seats on the right side in the back, providing us with storage space when accessibility isn't needed. Moreover, the wheelchair lift enables us to load carts full of food onto the bus—a huge time and back saver.

Fran Shepherd, a reading teacher at Price's Fork Elementary, suggested that we offer books on the bus. We jumped at this additional opportunity. Why not feed kids' minds along with their bodies? She rallied teachers and other personnel to serve as volunteer librarians and organized a team to manage the mobile backpack library. Shepherd enjoyed volunteering and "appreciated the opportunity in the summer of 2013 to take books on the Micah's Mobile Backpack bus." We overcame another hurdle when a church member with a commercial driver's license heard we needed a bus driver and signed up to drive every route. He came early to load the bus and stayed late to unload and clean up. His dedication made a real difference in the safe operation of the mobile backpack.

In addition to the city stops like the one described at the beginning of the story, we tried establishing a rural location. However, after three weeks of driving there and sitting for an hour with no kids in sight, I relearned the lesson that a central location with free food is not helpful for food insecure families who lack reliable transportation. I eliminated the stop, and we focused our time and efforts where we were reaching kids: on their doorsteps. Similarly, although we had a stop at the town's library, it drew only two or three children each week. I want to reach more families with a central downtown location. I am hopeful that in the coming summers, children without transportation will walk or use public transportation to get to the library, and families with vehicles will continue to come.

Micah's Mobile Backpack grew during the summer of 2015, when we provided more than 10,600 meals and shared 446 pounds of kid-friendly fruits and vegetables such as beans, blueberries, carrots, corn, peas, and tomatoes. We also partnered with a second elementary school to provide books and teacher and administrator contact in June and July.

Micah's Mobile Backpack has already had a substantial impact on the people in our community, both those served and those who do the serving. At one mobile home park, we fed nineteen children during our first visit. By August 2014, an average of fifty-two children from toddlers to high schoolers greeted us each week when they stepped out their front door to visit the bus drove up. As a consequence, as Pastor John relates, the volunteers for Micah's Mobile Backpack have a "much more personal" experience with the challenges of food security and community engagement. Unlike the school-year program, where volunteers have no contact with the students being helped, during the summer "you are packing a bag of food for a specific student based on their order from the week before. You go to the students' neighborhood, and you have the opportunity to hand them their bag of food, engage them in conversation, and get a small glimpse of how the gift of food makes a difference in their lives.

With a tremendous amount of support and dedication from volunteers and partners, Micah's Mobile Backpack has begun to achieve its goals. Fewer kids in our community suffer from summertime food insecurity. We have developed relationships, and our efforts are helping to strengthen our local community and beyond. So come June, we will stock the shelves with food, recruit volunteers, and gas up the bus to begin another journey with food for the body, mind, and soul. I know we will be making a difference. Micah's Mobile Backpack proves that reducing summertime food insecurity for school-aged kids is possible.

I am excited to think about the long-term ripple effects of our program as other folks hear about what we've done and explore ways to replicate and expand the mobile backpack program in their communities. We know of no other hunger relief agency that offers what Micah's Mobile Backpack does—yet. Within a few years, I hope that we will no longer be alone, and the food-security issues of children in other communities will be advanced by our success.

Micah's Soup for Seniors

We arrive a little early despite the ten-minute drive on a two-lane, winding back road. Seven smiling older adults stroll around the lobby of their fixed-income apartment building as we pull up. A couple stand off on their own, and a few more have gathered in a group. As I pull the large glass door open to enter, a strong breeze nudges me in.

"Ohhh, it's cold," says one of the women. I smile and agree. It's January, with temperatures dipping and snow coming from the northeast. The folks in the lobby and I chat about the weather while volunteers begin to bring in the food.

The residents rub their hands and smile as they watch Pastor John bring in large bins full of bags with a variety of breads and a few cookies. Eyes light up, and a few people move toward the delivery bench and begin sorting. The bench becomes a sharing and gathering spot. I am remembering the wonderful smell from a short while ago when the loaves were being sliced and the treats divided into portions.

The conversation turns to the merits of bagels: "I prefer the loaves to the bagels," says one resident, adding, "Really, I'm just happy to have the bread. It's so delicious!" Her fellow seniors nod and concur. We move on to ways to prepare the bagels to make them less bulky and easier to chew. A volunteer suggests cutting them really thin and briefly toasting them. The loaf lover nods her head as though she's never considered that option. Many of the residents point out bags that contain their pre-ferred items.

While we are inside talking and sorting, two high-school-aged volunteers are bringing in shopping carts loaded with bagged food. One spry resident joins them and wheels in the last cart. The high school boys begin to organize the food distribution in a small room off the lobby. They know the drill—they've been regular volunteers since the program's inception. They sort the bags into piles by the residents' names and floors. Then the boys grab clipboards with Pastor John and get ready to help the residents fill out menus for the following month. This month, everyone gets a large box of cereal since a partner group conducted a cereal drive for Micah's Soup for Seniors. "I'm not sure I can eat a whole box," one resident confides, "although I'm really happy to have it. I think I'll see if my neighbor wants to share. Then it won't go to waste." We agree that's a great plan.

As the first group begins to fill out menus, other residents start to arrive in the lobby. Most pause and look over the bagged bread before moving on to give their orders for next time. Residents chat with the volunteers, asking how they are doing and thanking them for their helpfulness. There's a sense of familiar fellowship. Resident Bonita Sarver declares, "Micah's Soup for Seniors in awesome. It's a shame when folks have to choose between food and medicine. I look forward to the food, and I'm glad they always bring the applesauce or fruit I put on my menu."

Within forty-five minutes, the bags have been distributed, and a couple of residents have been cajoled into taking two bags of baked goods back with them to their apartment. They don't want people to think they are taking too much food. The volunteers park the empty shopping carts in the lobby and wave good-bye. The remaining residents wave back and say, "See you next month." We load up the empty bins and head home.

Earlier in the evening, I had entered the fellowship hall at St. Michael and encountered another group of volunteers whistling and humming as they set up tables in a circle. The atmosphere is jovial, and these six volunteers, too, have the routine down pat. We've been doing this for twenty-eight months and have shared more than twenty-five hundred bags of food.

We started because, as Pastor John explains, "I was watching a news report about another feeding program that gave food to seniors once over the summer, and it occurred to me that we could do an end-of-the-month distribution to bridge folks over til their next social security check arrives." So since September 2012 volunteers have been gathering on the fourth Tuesday of every month to pack and then deliver food to low-resource seniors. Collectively, our volunteers have invested more than nine hundred hours of their time in the program.

Down the corridor, four volunteers are slicing and bagging the donated bread. Conversation turns to college basketball, with friendly ribbing about rival schools and endless speculation about who'll do well in the national tournament. The teasing shows the camaraderie among the volunteers.

Back in the fellowship hall, the first table holds three color-coded piles of menus filled out the previous month. The colors represent the three different apartment complexes, helping to keep the deliveries organized. Ninety senior adults living in income-restricted housing have filled out a menu, selecting from a variety of canned soups, cereals, fruits, and vegetables plus rice, peanut butter, and beans. There's space to jot down special requests, which our volunteer shoppers do their best to honor when funding and availability allow.

Food is arranged in groups on the tables: soups together; pasta, oatmeal, and cereal; different kinds of fruit cups; corn, peas, and mixed vegetables; tuna; and peanut butter. By the time setup has finished, twenty volunteers are on hand. Each volunteer grabs a menu and begins a circuit around the tables, carefully selecting the items marked and placing them in a bag. Lines of volunteers wind around both the inside and the outside of the circle of tables, so there's a lot of conversation while the bags are being filled. Sandy Birch, who is retired from Virginia Tech and is a part-time lay associate at St. Michael, says that she volunteers with Soup for Seniors because "it's my thing."

When the bags are filled, they go to husband-and-wife volunteers Jody and Doug Smiley, who tie the handles into tight knots and staple on the menus. Doug says he volunteers in part because he likes "organizing things" and more importantly because "I see this as filling a void for seniors and also really like the local outreach part of it." He and Jody hand the bags to the youth volunteers, who load them onto metal carts. When the carts are full, the bags will be taken out to the vehicles that will bring the food to the senior housing complex.

When all the cars are loaded, the group splits up, with about half of the volunteers heading out to deliver the food. Everyone else stays behind to count and record the leftover items so the volunteer coordinator will know what is already on hand when she prepares next month's grocery order. Then the volunteers put away the tables and say their good-byes.

As with the other outreach programs sponsored by St. Michael, Micah's Soup for Seniors has no religious requirements for the volunteers or the recipients. However, spiritual opportunities sometimes present themselves and are acted on at a participant's request. Remembered one volunteer, "One of the recipients of Micah's Soup for Seniors, after receiving her bag of food, expressed some disappointment that we didn't have a church service, too. So we led a prayer session for a few minutes; we all held hands. It was a nice little moment and came very naturally to us as part of this important ministry."

Micah's Closet

The volunteer shopper looked over the information for the little girl in the Head Start preschool program. Then, sitting at her kitchen table with pencil and paper, she started to plan: five short-sleeved shirts and seven shorts or skirts—one girly skirt for special occasions, two skorts (so the girl could hang upside down on the monkey bars at school), and four pairs of shorts. A pink hooded sweatshirt, since mornings and evenings were still chilly even though the calendar said it was spring. Socks—some frilly ones, some sportier—and pajamas and underwear. No need to get shoes—the local running store would provide them. Fifteen minutes later, she was organized for Micah's Closet to begin to help clothe another low-resource child.

The next step was coming up with a shopping strategy. She checked the Sunday newspaper circulars for sales at local stores and made a note to see what they had. She also browsed clothes online, hoping to take advantage of a gift card donated by a friend of Micah's Closet. Any items that the Micah's Closet shopper couldn't find locally would be ordered and shipped.

This woman was one of a dozen shoppers for the spring distribution of Micah's Closet. Volunteer coordinator Sheila McCartan had given the shoppers information regarding each participating child's age and clothing sizes as well as his or her favorite colors and characters. Likewise she shared a budget estimate per child and the springtime list of clothing items.

Armed with the information about the sales, the shopper headed out the following Saturday. At her first stop, she made her way to the young girls' section and began to comb through the racks. Right away, she found two short-sleeved pink-and-purple collared shirts with flowers. She thought of her own niece and decided they were perfect—a little bit fancy, but not too delicate for everyday wear. Next she spied a display with more practical t-shirts and selected three of them. Khaki, light blue, and denim skorts and shorts, too, were easy to find. A four-pack of girly socks and another of athletic socks went into the cart. Less than an hour after she'd arrived at the store, she was done, having checked most of the items off her list.

Pleased with her progress, she headed across the divided highway to her second stop. Success! She found a hooded sweatshirt with flowers on the back marked down to less than five dollars. She was almost finished shopping and hadn't even used the gift card.

Later in the week, she took a few minutes while dinner was in the oven and got back on the Internet. A few clicks and her online cart held two packages of girls' undergarments and two pairs of pajamas. Grand total: $115 out of the Micah's Closet budget, plus a gift card that would otherwise most likely have lain forgotten in a drawer. A small investment of the shopper's time and energy had provided a child with much-needed clothes—and not just in the right sizes, but in colors and patterns she liked.

This was not the volunteer shopper's first experience with Micah's Closet. She had participated during the preceding fall. She was pleased to discover that she was getting better at it—she had spent less money this season. And she found that others, too, responded positively: "The store clerks who may ask if I need help finding anything are interested and excited to learn about the program." On one occasion, another shopper recalled, "I was buying jeans for a young man. I explained to the clerk about Micah's Closet, and she reduced the price of the jeans and also gave me her store discount." Small acts of kindness like these happen often when volunteers share the Micah's Closet story.

Other volunteers also enjoy shopping for Micah's Closet. One says, "I find that the store clerks that may ask if I need help finding anything are interested and excited to learn about the program. I was happy to hear the quotes we heard from the grateful children, their parents, and their teachers. Since we don't actually see them, it is nice to hear the positive feedback." Another volunteer points out, "Because I can engage my 8-year old granddaughter in the project we shop for clothing together for her age group. She's my consultant."

Prior to the program's creation, many children from low-resource families in our community got clothing from charity closets and similar low-cost retailers of used clothing. Others got by with hand-me-downs, sometimes ill-fitting or threadbare. Micah's Caring Initiative volunteers created Micah's Closet after realizing that caring about children in our community meant providing quality clothing as well as feeding them. Over the past two years, we have given clothing to eighty-seven preschoolers and elementary school students, including some with special needs. Students are referred to us from our local community services board.

I was recently out running errands and ran into a grandmother I recognized from the Micah's Mobile Backpack route. She greeted me with a huge smile and we hugged each other. Then she pulled out photos of her preschool-aged granddaughter wearing the clothes she received from Micah's Closet. For five minutes we scrolled through the pictures together. In every snapshot, the four-year-old beamed. As I commented on how happy she looked, her grandmother thanked me and described how the clothing made her granddaughter feel special. I went on my way feeling grateful.

Other families with children who participate in the program share similar stories, and this appreciation helps to inspire Micah's Closet coordinator McCartan. She chose to become involved with Micah's Closet because the "program hits home with me personally.... New clothes for school weren't always in the cards for me as a kid. I wore a lot of hand-me-downs, and having followed two brothers, the clothes weren't always *girl* appropriate. I remember how special I felt when I did get something of my own."

We initially conceived of Micah's Closet as distributing clothes during the first week of school so that participants would begin the school year with new outfits. However, school staff suggested that a seasonal distribution would not only provide warm clothes in the winter and lighter clothes for the spring but also "rally the community for the outreach."

After the shopping is done, volunteers gather at St. Michael to prepare their purchases for distribution by faculty and staff at our partner schools and agencies. Having the school staff or social workers share the gifts of clothing helps us maintain confidentiality. Like the other Micah's Caring Initiative programs, Micah's Closet welcomes everyone to share their gifts of time, skill, and financial support. In 2015, the program distributed 1,784 articles of clothing to 123 kids!

CHAPTER 3
Helping

Focusing on People's Connections and Assets

H elping programs like Micah's Caring Initiative succeed as a consequence of ample resources in a variety of forms. Individuals and groups with strong social capital succeed more often than those with weak social connections. Social capital, a web of relationships, provides connection, belonging, and a sense of community. Individuals, groups, and communities need both bonding and bridging capital to succeed. Bonding social capital tends to result in stronger relationships within a group while bridging social capital goes between groups resulting in wider social bonds. Interfaith communities also tend to build more of bonding and bridging capital than other organizations.

Helping initiatives also succeed more when they focus on the assets of individuals, groups, and communities instead of their deficits. This sort of focus requires paying attention to and leveraging a community's resources, culture, tradition, history, experience and skills, time, and peer groups. Most asset-based community engagement starts by discovering the strengths possessed by people and the groups to which they belong, using these assets to build reciprocal and beneficial partnerships to bring about change, and then continuing to build new relationships outside the immediate community.

Volunteers comprise a critical asset for the success of community-based helping programs. To attract, retain, and grow volunteers requires creating a welcoming climate, meaningful experiences, and strong support for success. The most effective volunteer experiences focus on the task at hand and on developing volunteers and the organization through a people-centered, process-oriented learning environment.

In fact, many volunteer opportunities create new and deeper relationships that help people change the way they see the world and then in turn deepen their volunteer service.

Micah's Backpack and its spin-off programs focus on feeding and clothing friends and neighbors while building a stronger community. This two-pronged mission appeals to our volunteers. We connect different segments of the local population interested in making a difference while improving our community as a whole. Overall, the community-based model allows us to tap into the wisdom of the group and the resources of many people and organizations.

Micah's Backpack distinguishes itself from many other backpack feeding programs because of our community-based method of alleviating food insecurity. Most backpack organizations pair one interfaith or civic group and one school. Our approach provides a holistic exchange across groups and needs while building community within the Micah's Caring Initiative and our town. By engaging our neighbors in sharing their time and talents, we encourage them to make the community a better place. People who participate in Micah's Caring Initiative help build social capital by making and using new connections, engaging with people from different backgrounds, and strengthening a sense of community around important purposes. Everyone becomes a stakeholder in feeding and clothing our neighbors while building the capacity of our nonprofit organizations. We strengthen connections by working together to improve others' lives and in so doing improve our own lives as volunteers. Longtime Micah's Backpack participant Stacie Castro says she and her husband "volunteer because of the people. We love how Micah's Backpack has volunteers from all areas and walks of life. On any given Thursday, we have the opportunity to interact with kids from the age of five all the way up to ninety-five."

Our community has many organizations that rely on volunteers, and Micah's Backpack offers a unique opportunity. According to John Kell, a college professor,

> I think most of my volunteering in the past has been more self-serving—e.g., I've volunteered in Scouts because my son is in Scouts.... This is different

because it involves serving people I don't even know. It's really much more in the spirit of community service than the other things I've done. Also, there is a wider variety of people that volunteer compared to other groups I've been in. Students from elementary school, retired adults, and every age in between are represented. People from all over the world are present. One night, a group from VT showed up and there were 37 countries represented. I spent an hour talking to a woman from the Ukraine.

Soon after we started Micah's Backpack, we discovered that a major reason people share their time and resources with the program comes from the sense of community created by the volunteer experience. Kathy Duong, a two year student intern, reports,

Being a Micah's Backpack intern has been extremely rewarding not only because I get to help the Blacksburg community, but also because the community atmosphere is extraordinary. Everyone who works and volunteers with Micah's is always so thankful for the effort we put in to make this program work and very encouraging. Small acts like that let me know that my skills are recognized, and is the reason why I love working with Micah's Backpack!

During our Thursday night packing sessions, volunteers wear nametags, enabling people to address each other by name. It's a simple thing, and it helps ensure that no one is a stranger. To keep people from getting bored while waiting their turn and to help start conversations, we ask trivia questions of the group. As the Micah's Backpack coordinator, my job on Thursday nights is hospitality: I walk around, greet volunteers, introduce people, and help them make connections. We welcome young and young at heart, sprinters and marathoners. Because people do not have to make a continuous commitment to the packing sessions, they come when doing so is convenient. People who are sick or have to stay late at work don't have to worry about finding someone to fill in for them—they just don't come that week. This approach provides a flexibility that people really appreciate.

Many of the packing tasks are simple and appropriate for even very young children. We have had many people who began volunteering for a mandatory middle school service project and have continued to come long after they were required to do so. By the time these volunteers are in high school, their Micah's Backpack packing experiences have changed the way they view community service. Bright Zheng, a high schooler, explains, "Micah's Backpack is my first long-term community service. I used to think that community service or volunteering is merely an assignment, but after I started Micah's Backpack, my definition of volunteering changed from an assignment to an activity that helps our community."

One of our middle school volunteers told me that she was receiving our gifts of food. When she came to help pack, however, she saw herself as relatively fortunate: "My participation in Micah's Backpack opened my eyes to the lack of care some children in Blacksburg receive, and the poverty and trouble many families face." In addition, "Participating in Micah's Backpack made my family realize how lucky we were and it gave us a way to contribute to the community that loved and supported us so much."

Other volunteers participate because they see the immediate results of their time commitment. According to Priscilla Baker of the Blacksburg Newcomers' Club,

> Our members like to help with Micah's Backpack because it is a low time commitment with a high return of satisfaction. They really feel like they are doing something that immediately helps those in their own community that is very important to our members, rather than just supporting national organizations. And the sense of community created at the church while packing the bags provides another layer of fulfillment and enjoyment.

Angela Little, director of the Retired Senior Volunteer Program (RSVP) concurs. Volunteers from her group "want to support Micah's Backpack because it helps the children in our area combat hunger and they ... enjoy the camaraderie of working with many other volunteers and groups when packing the bags with food. MBP is very well organized and appreciative of all who give time to support their mission." Similarly, Jane Carr, who works with an interfaith group that provides Micah's Backpack with volunteers and financial gifts and conducts food drives, reports,

> My church's volunteers enjoy the time they donate to this program because it also allows them the opportunity to interact with the Virginia Tech and Radford University students as well as with various other groups from the community that we otherwise would not have an opportunity to meet.

While we pack and socialize, we experience that good feeling that we are doing what God instructed us to do, small though it may be.

Sarah Brooks, a former intern, sums up this interconnected impact when she writes, "Because of the community's enthusiastic engagement with this problem, many children have consistently been sent home with meals for the weekends. So, I would say that I now see more than ever before how crucial community engagement is to addressing the issues with the population of any community."

Michelle Barton volunteers on packing nights not only as a way to strengthen the larger community but also as a team-building exercise for her coworkers. In her words, Micah's Backpack,

> struck a chord with so many people that the turnout from work [to volunteer] has been amazing. During my pitch to the group we had some tears and immediately the questions of how we could help came up. It's amazing to see everyone pitching ideas of how to streamline our donations and ideas for what to donate. So services like this, and its ability to get everyone revved up to help, inspire me.

At Micah's Backpack, we encourage volunteers to do what they want to be doing. For example, someone who enjoys counting can choose to work in inventory. Someone who likes being funny and chatting with others can manage crowd control at the front of the packing line or reading the trivia questions, keeping the atmosphere light and engaging volunteers waiting their turn. Lisa Acciai became our volunteer graphic designer after finding the Thursday night packing sessions a little too crowded for her taste. This way, her contribution not only takes advantage of her particular skills but occurs in a comfortable setting. She says,

> I share my graphic design skills because it's important to me to give back to the community... rather than just donating money to a charity where I don't have a lot of control over how the money is spent. I would rather personally contribute my time and talent to causes that I believe in and can see a direct impact of my efforts.

Similarly, people who work during the day can participate in our evening packing sessions, while people with evening commitments that prevent them from packing can

assist with Friday morning food deliveries. In short, as Rachel Hosig says, "Micah's Backpack definitely recognizes the skills that each individual has to offer. There is an opportunity here for anyone who wants to help."

By creating a flexible and welcoming atmosphere and by striving to let everyone who wants to help find a way to do so, Micah's Backpack has a positive impact on its volunteers as well as on the kids we feed. We have had great success recruiting and retaining volunteers. They tell others about their positive experiences and share our story. This word of mouth, in turn, moves more people to offer their time and financial support, creating a cycle of positive change that both feeds hungry kids and builds a better and stronger community.

CHAPTER 4
Engaging

Focus on the Common Good

We started our program by providing food for five hungry children and it didn't take long to realize that decreasing food insecurity in our community required deep engagement for the common good. We learned that relationships built around a common goal were important for bringing the right partners and volunteers into the project. We have been very intentional about who we work with and why. We found that not everyone fits the Micah's Caring Initiative style of gracious and thankful leadership. It also became clear that protecting the Micah's Caring brand sometimes needs to trump personal feelings and motivations. For example, leadership for each program within the Initiative must fully embrace the Caring brand. This sometimes creates uncomfortable situations when a volunteer's vision does not fit with Micah's culture. We've learned that our best Micah's Caring Initiative leaders defer most praise and accept more fault than they deserve. When these leaders put the health and mission of the organization above all else, then others involved tend to mirror that attitude and behavior.

One program had some issues getting off the ground when one of the founders had some disagreements with other organizers about how the program should operate. As Pastor John recalls, "The broader ministry had a vision of how things are accomplished, that vision helped the individual to have the passion to get it going, and then in the implementation she discovered the partnership approach with the school didn't fit the model she envisioned. Ensuing conflict over the implementation led to a change in leadership." At other times, volunteers have suggested taking Micah's Backpack in directions that clashed with our core values. Despite the good intentions—and potentially good ideas—of these volunteers, we opted to stick with our model rather than change our approach. We cannot be all things to all people, and some outreach initiatives are simply not right for us. We expect our leaders and other volunteers to embrace our way of doing things, and if they cannot agree with us, we encourage them to find other volunteer opportunities that fit them more comfortably. We strive to stay focused on serving the community, not ourselves by modeling and nurturing our ideals and values.

It is important to put time and resources into getting the right people engaged in leadership and volunteer roles the first time to prevent directing lots of energy into issues later on. However, it is also never too late to make the right decisions about the best use of resources for the success of the Initiative and the community. Waiting to find a better leader, volunteer, or partner fit can compromise short and long term effectiveness. We've learned that an action orientation to staying closely aligned with our common goal across all aspects of the Initiative saves time and energy, and enhances our reputation and effectiveness.

Engaging deeply with community to address a major issue is complex and multifaceted. We found it takes extra effort for volunteers to understand how all the programs operate and that they comprise one overarching initiative. They most often tend to know about Micah's Backpack, the original and most developed program in the Initiative. One volunteer says, "When I say I go to St. Michael, people have said, 'Oh, that is the Micah's Backpack Church.' Most haven't connected the other ministries yet. However, when I start talking about Micah's Closet, I always ask if they have heard of Micah's Backpack, a high percentage say yes, then I let them know they fall under the same umbrella of caring for the community and share the story of all the outreach programs and how they fed off of Micah's Backpack." To help people appropriately engage with the Initiative, we must continue to be vigilant about demonstrating the importance of all the Initiative's programs.

Early in the creation of the Initiative we determined a small and clear set of indicators for success to measure and share with the community and other stakeholders as the project grew. We found it important to keep track of the number of meals we provided, the amount of garden produce and other food provided, the number of students and schools we served, and the amount of money raised to support the effort. To show our impact on community engagement we also consistently collected information on the number of volunteers involved in the Initiative and the number of hours they served. These statistics over time helped keep the community, partners, volunteers, and participants engaged with the intended common good of the Initiative and take pride in their role in its success.

In many ways, our work together has become visible as a form of community engagement that not only addresses hunger but also promotes human and organizational development. We believe it is critical to meet our volunteers where they are by giving them opportunities for personal growth and learning from interaction with each other, being flexible with expectations, and providing opportunities that allow people to contribute their particular skills in comfortable ways. The community has become more deeply engaged in this work because we provide opportunities to share a low amount of time but with a high level of satisfaction for those we serve and ourselves.

We've learned the importance of growing our own leaders who have experienced our caring brand and values. As leaders in the wings they know what it is like to serve others, be engaged for the common good, and are familiar with our ways of getting things done and how we relate to each other. This internal leadership development pathway helps volunteers and partners stretch and build their own capacities as well as affirm their current valuable experience, skills, and interests. We specifically look for individuals to lead our engagement who see the whole without losing sight of the details, share their wisdom humbly, live intentionally, take calculated risks, maintain self-awareness and accountability, relate positively with others, and have integrity.

We have discovered over and over again how motivating it is to show care for each other in our community directly. We intentionally weave an ethic of caring and hospitality into our community engagement and hunger relief efforts. Our volunteers and partners are motivated deeply by directly seeing the results of their support and being close to those we serve. Micah's Caring Initiative has realized the strong motivation of focusing on local impact in a community by caring for our neighbors in a variety of ways. We strive to live fully in relationship with each other in a way that puts forward our best selves, to see each other's lives as part of our own, and to be creative and sensitive rather than judgmental. We provide resources for and expect our projects leaders, partners, and volunteers to be architects of caring environments of warmth, acceptance, and trust working to address the common goal of alleviating hunger for our low-resource families.

CHAPTER 5
Connecting

Church Is for Worship and Community Engagement

I n many ways, the St. Michael Lutheran Church congregation serves as a catalyst for organizing the community. According to Pastor John, "From a community standpoint, Micah's Backpack is far and away our most visible and well known ministry to people in the community. Micah's Backpack has helped make St. Michael a legend on the community grapevine for helping our neighbors." Although recognition springs from the outreach of Micah's Backpack, the initial support of the church and congregational culture fostered the programs' successes. According to him, Lutheran theology is conducive to outreach programs like Micah's Backpack. He says,

> As Lutherans, we believe that God's gift of love is a free gift, we no strings attached. This understanding of God's grace, God's unconditional love, mercy and forgiveness, inspires us to share God's gift of love freely with others. God has blessed us with a variety of gifts that gives us the opportunity to put those gifts to work blessing others.

By focusing our call to help people in need, instead of the need to convert people to a specific set of religious beliefs, St. Michael and Micah's Backpack connect with other Christian groups, non-Christian groups and corporate partners in a way that some religious sponsored helping organizations have not been able to do. This willingness to see love of neighbor as an activity inspired by a set of beliefs, not as an end to spreading religious beliefs allows St. Michael and many Lutheran organizations to be more flexible and adaptable in creating partnerships and implementing programs which make a difference in the lives of people in need.

The Micah's Caring Initiative Programs grew out of the Lutheran love for our neighbors that St. Michael embodies. For example, the congregation hosts an annual Thanksgiving meal for anyone who wants to attend. Diners include members of the congregation, international students, and area residents. Lately, the meal feeds 190 people in this two decade old community caring event. Local businesses donate cutlery and some food items, and we prepare and provide the rest of the meal.

St Michael maintains other strong traditions of helping neighbors. Multiple Girl Scout and Boy Scout troops meet in the fellowship hall. The congregation also created and generously supports a Justice and Mercy Fund that pays for utilities, fuel, or medication for local residents who need help. A Mother's Morning Out Program provides childcare and a nursery school environment for two-to four-year-olds. For many years, the congregation hosted SHARE, a food cooperative program that became part of Micah's Soup for Seniors. We also partner with a local child-care provider to offer an early Head Start program at the church focused on low-resource children ages six weeks to three years.

Love for our neighbors drives what St Michael does. We help our friends and neighbors by feeding and clothing them and by offering opportunities to have meaningful, positive impact on the lives of others. In both cases, there are no religious requirements for our activities together. Participants and volunteers exist on all points of the spectrum from believers to nonbelievers. This flexibility and respect for people's values helps us expand the church from simply being a location for worship to one that is also an energizing community engagement hub.

St. Michael fosters the growth of Micah's Caring Initiative in a few important ways. First, the congregational leadership recognized that supporting strong coordinators helps strengthen the outreach and impact of the programs. In my case, they understood that the work I did 10-15 hours each week to manage, grow, and represent the program should be a salaried position. The other Initiative programs are less intensely hands-on so a group of dedicated volunteers rather than paid staff lead and manage the activities and relationships.

The congregation embraces the use of the church building as a hub for community engagement activities. On any given packing night at St. Michael, there may be as many volunteers present as there are worshippers on a Sunday morning. As Pastor John points out,

> St. Michael houses two congregations one that gathers for worship and a congregation that gathers for service. The worshipping congregation is made up of about 350 unique individuals and on any given Sunday about 130 of them show up for a worship service. The serving congregation is made up of about 700 unique individuals and on any given Thursday night about 80 of them show up to live out their call to serve others.

This hospitality of sharing the church space with others resonates with members and non-members interested in community engagement and love for neighbors. This sharing attitude directly impacts Micah's Backpack's ability to partner with over 250 community organizations to address the needs local individuals, families, and organizations. The group understands that we need to get to know and learn about each other, create opportunities for deeper relationships, reduce isolation, and share our resources to break down barriers to work together to improve our community.

St. Michael has put in place many important connecting elements needed for successful community-based organizations. Specifically church leaders invest effort and resources into understanding the importance, implementation, and impact of their role as a hub of community engagement. In many ways they have been engaging in a thought and action experiment related to further defining their mission of who they are and how they want to show it. These leaders and the program coordinators they support are also optimistic about their role in community engagement including being willing to make changes-even unpopular or uncomfortable changes to be a better community engagement hub. They have realistic expectations for success and resist pressures and politics to stick with the status quo or easy routes to engagement or dealing with difficult situations. Finally the whole congregation is open to self-awareness, growth, and conflict as important ways to better serve as a center for community engagement.

Blacksburg resembles many rural university communities with countless organizations addressing community issues. However, Blacksburg succeeds effectively in improving the quality of life because organizations like St. Michael provide an anchor or backbone institution to holistically, comprehensively, and catalytically address issues. This allows St. Michael to serve as an effective and efficient central host and resource hub for the whole community around one specific issue. A central hub also helps more fully develop cultural, political, social, financial, built, human, and natural capital through its comprehensive approach to a community issue. Government organizations and private businesses tend to lack this ability or mission to be a hub that focuses so tightly on an issue. St. Michael as hub and anchor institution makes it more likely that program gaps disappear and overlap and repetition decline. As an easily recognizable center of community activity around a specific issue, a diverse group of individuals, families, and partners find it easy to get involved in their community in ways that fit their own needs while helping reach an important community goal.

A St. Michael member and elementary school teacher, Maggie Maloney, sees the role of the church as a hub for community engagement directly when she says, "I definitely encounter people in the community who recognize our church as the Micah's church. As a teacher, I am very aware of its impact on local children!" As a congregation St Michael embraces this recognition and celebrate the ways the Micah's Caring Initiative programs make a difference in the lives of the people who encounter them. We are proud of our role as a catalyzing nucleus for community engagement.

CHAPTER 6
Listening and Learning

Those We Serve Teach Us

We've learned that we most successfully meet the needs of low-resource families and youth when we involve them in decisions about our programs. We have discovered over and over again that coordinators, volunteers, and partners don't fully understand the lived experience of our low-resource families. Going directly to our program participants to determine the best approach to program logistics saves time and resources and make our programs much more effective.

A hallmark of the Micah's Caring Initiative programs has been a willingness to hear what others have to say and to learn from their experiences, observations, and advice. Staff and volunteer coordinators listen actively to suggestions from volunteers and those we serve. For example, we offer families of the children we feed through Micah's Backpack the opportunity to give us feedback, generally through online surveys but also more directly.

If parents provide an email address on their child's Micah's Backpack program participation permission slip, we use an online survey to gather information anonymously. In 2013, 10 out of 65 parents completed an online survey. In 2015, 12 parents filled out the online survey and 21 participated in the phone survey. Of these parents 31 said their child was less hungry because of Micah's Backpack. Additionally, one parent shared that her son stays hungry due to his ADHD medication. Micah's Backpack weekend food helps decrease the frequent hunger from his medication. For many low-resource families' access to telephone and internet service may not be very reliable and that in turn affects our ability to gather data.

Even though we do not get feedback from the majority of the parents of youth in this program, we still find the information and advice very helpful in shaping our efforts.

We learned from the parent surveys, for example, that we were sending home too much peanut butter. It never occurred to us that too much peanut butter would be a problem since it is generally popular and nutritious. Families reported that they had multiple jars of peanut butter in their cupboards. In response, we reduced the frequency of peanut butter gifts from every other week to once a month, a change that incidentally provided a cost savings for us. Similarly, when we included only cans of mixed vegetables, parents reported in our survey that their kids preferred to have a single veggie each week. Subsequently, we began a weekly rotation of corn, peas, and carrots. Listening to others, therefore, enabled us to better serve our community and also to reallocate our resources to other areas.

Although we have limited opportunities to receive direct feedback from families served by Micah's Backpack during the school year, the mobile backpack program is very different. The volunteers on the bus frequently get to know children and their families, and asking them questions about the program naturally occurs. Likewise Pastor John reports "Soup for Seniors participants have shaped the process by giving feedback on the menu."

We also welcome opinions and suggestions from volunteers. We are open to trying new ideas consistent with our mission that might help us to become better at what we do. When a volunteer who is an engineer suggested that a different pattern for packing food might simplify the process, we tried his approach and found immediate benefits. At one time, we had quality control volunteers who checked the items in the food bags to make sure that they had been filled correctly. After several other volunteers confided that they didn't like people looking over their shoulders while they worked and one said that leaving the bag untied made her feel like she hadn't completed the process, we eliminated the checking. Instead, we trust that our volunteers do their best and it is good enough. The volunteers filling the bags take pride in what they are doing, and that is all the quality control we need.

By taking this approach, we help volunteers engage fully with the process and enjoy their participation. As Pastor John notes, "we let the people on the ground run with their ideas."

In turn, we provide our stakeholders with feedback on what they have helped us accomplish. Each month, we publish "Sharing the Story," a report in which we let our volunteers and partner agencies know what their support has enabled us to do. Each report includes data and graphics, providing concrete information such as year-to-date totals for number of volunteer hours and meals provided as well as visual representations of our impact. These reports allow people to see the big picture—the enormous enterprise that can result from a lot of people contributing however they can.

Once Micah's Backpack became established in our community, we discovered the possibilities for additional outreach by continuing to listen. Feeding senior adults living in limited-income housing seemed like a natural extension of a youth backpack feeding program. So, too, did creating a space for communally raising vegetables and fruits to share with our community. Summertime feeding was a logical progression from the academic year feeding. These additional programs helped enhance our contribution to the public good through improved quality of life for our low-resource neighbors.

Recognizing the value of the advice, observations, and support our existing and potential partners made these new programs feasible. People want to support programs that take their thoughts into consideration, value their ideas and efforts, celebrate their skills, and make their community a better place to live. In every case we try to put the needs of the community above individual interests of any staff or volunteer. In fact, we often see great growth in volunteers who discover how their own interests are aligned with the greater good.

In rare instances, volunteers have taken advantage of our flexible structure to bully others and fail to remember that we are not experts. When this has happened, I've listened to the impacted volunteers and asked them to change their style. In a couple of cases, the volunteers have been unable or unwilling to modify their behavior. I've had to ask them not to come back, though I always offer to meet them for coffee to discuss the Micah's Caring Initiative philosophy further. In these cases it's best for us to part ways so they can find another outlet comfortable with their approach to volunteering and we can continue to operate as an open and welcoming volunteer environment for everyone.

We've learned a variety of lessons from listening to and learning from our program participants, volunteers, and partners. Sometimes we are frustrated that we've been unable to expand or improve our programs after trying a variety of approaches that we thought would succeed. Often, our stakeholders help us realize that we are addressing the symptoms of the problem rather than the root causes. By getting to the source of the issues many of the symptoms go away. For example we thought bringing Micah's Mobile Backpack sites would thrive until our partners helped us realize we chose the sites and families knew they were unsafe and didn't show up. When we listed to the families about their need for safety instead of our needs or perceptions, participation increased dramatically.

We've discovered that we need to listen to and learn from others in a variety of ways. Getting information about program improvements from several sources allows us to see more clearly common issues and potential solutions. We continue to remember that we need to ask people for information in ways that are convenient for them, not convenient for us as program coordinators and hosts.

Listening and Learning in Multiple Ways

Method	Who	What	Active Learning
Online and written surveys	Parents	Menus, impacts	Provide less of some items and more of others, reduce costs, alleviate hunger, improve health
Email	Parents	Menus, impacts	Improve item selection
Phone survey	Parents	Menus, impacts	Improve item selection

Method	Who	What	Active Learning
Face-to-face conversations	Stakeholders (participants, families, volunteers, funders)	Processes, impacts	More efficient packing and delivery of food, expansion of programs
Observations	Coordinators and volunteers	Processes, impacts	Personal development
Case Studies	Volunteers	Impacts	Change perceptions about low-resource families

We pride ourselves in being a learning organization that intentionally and strategically seeks out, uses, and shares information to improve our processes, outcomes, and project environments. We learn not only from listening to others but we continue our learning as we put suggestions into action. One of the reasons for writing this book is to share what we've learned over the past several years about feeding programs for low-resource individuals and at the same time critically reflect on our efforts. We enjoy exploring and sharing promising practices and lessons learned while addressing hunger as a complex community issue.

Listening to and learning from our stakeholders requires us to be very open to other's ideas instead of our own, be creative, and to let go of our own assumptions about others. Doing things differently than we had intended may be a much better approach and we have to be humble enough to be comfortable with giving up a bit of ourselves and who we are to better serve others.

CHAPTER 7
Partnering

A University Embraces Hunger and Poverty Rather Than Ignoring It

We have greatly benefited from tapping into the wisdom and resources of many volunteers, partner organizations, and institutions. Our partnering network includes organizations and individuals from all sectors of our community. As the Initiative has expanded, so has our network as we seek new partners and new partners seek us. We specifically look for partners who can help us be local change leaders and who believe in our asset-based approach to change. We find that we connect and work best with people and organizations when they have a similar goal as ours, are in close proximity, or they have a particular specialty or set of resources that we need. We only engage with partners who believe in reciprocity of power, resources, respect, human and organizational development, ownership of success and failure, interdependence, leadership, and prestige.

Micah's Caring Initiative thrives because we coexist with Virginia Tech whose motto is *Ut Prosim*: That I May Serve. The university's students, faculty, and staff take that mission seriously by being excellent partners in helping our programs benefit the community. As a high resource partner, Virginia Tech helps us build multiple connections to deepen and widen our reach, visibility, legitimacy, and popularity. The university also gives us important access to technology, innovations, and helping hands. In turn, Virginia Tech as a publicly funded institution provides important public value in the community where it resides.

Micah's Caring Initiative Partners

Type of Partnership	Partners
Academic Partners	Blacksburg High School (BHS) A Better Community Club * BHS Agriculture Department * BHS Beta Club * BHS Culinary Arts Department * BHS Class of 2011 * BHS DECA * BHS Family and Consumer Science * BHS Habitat for Humanity * BHS Helping Hands Club * BHS SCO * Blacksburg Middle School (BMS) 8th Grade Civics 2011-2015 * BMS Theater Arts * Blacksburg New School * Gilbert Linkous Elementary School (GLES) PTO * Kipps Elementary School (KES) PTO * Price's Fork Elementary School (PFES) PTO * Rainbow Riders PTA * Tuxedo Pandas Robotics Team
Civic Partners	AARP-Blacksburg * All Arts, Science, Technology Camp * American Culinary Federation-NRV Chapter * American Legion Chapter * AMERICORPS VISTA * Blacksburg Farmer's Market * Blacksburg Junior Women's Club * Blacksburg Newcomer's Club * Blacksburg and Montgomery County Residents * Blacksburg Partnership * Blacksburg Rotary * Blacksburg Women's Club * Blacksburg United Methodist Pre School * Cub Scouts 704 * Dental Aid of NRV * Delta Sigma Theta Alumni Chapter * Downtown Blacksburg * Girl Scout Troop 396 * Girl Scout Troop 737 * Hunter's Lodge #156 * Montgomery-Blacksburg Kiwanis Club * MOPS at Blacksburg Christian Fellowship * MOPS at Blacksburg United Methodist Church * Leading Lights of the NRV * Leadership New River Valley Alumni * No Name Dames * New River Valley Association of Realtors * NRV Dental Partnership * Operation Santa Claus * Rotary of Blacksburg * RSVP of NRV * Runners Who Knit * Young Professional's Network of the New River Valley Association of Realtors
Collegiate Partners	A B PSci * African Student Association * AFROTC * Alpha Chi Omega * Alpha Epsilon Delta * Alpha Gamma Rho * Alpha Kappa Alpha * Alpha Kappa Psi * Alpha Omega Kappa * Alpha Phi Omega * Alpha Zeta * American Medical Student Association * Baptist Campus Ministries * Black Organization Council * Black Student Alliance * Campus Kitchens * Center for Academic Enrichment and Excellence

Type of Partnership	Partners
	* Chemistry Department * Chi Alpha * Chi Delta Alpha * Circle K International * College of Liberal Arts and Human Sciences at Virginia Tech (VT) * CommonWEALTH of Scholars * Community Nutrition Students * Continuing Professional Education Outreach and International Affairs * Cooper House * Corps of Cadets Hall Council * Dairy Club * Delta Psi Nu * Delta Sigma Theta * Empty Bowls *Epsilon Sigma Alpha * EGSP Fulbright * FarmHouse * Fashion Merchandising and Design Society * Fitness and Nutrition Club * Food Science Club * Freethinkers *Gamma Beta Phi * Golden Key * Honors Residential College * Humphreys Fellows 2012, 13, 14, 15 * Industrial Design * Hypatia the Female Engineering Living Learning Community * IMPACT at the University of Georgia * Industrial and Systems Engineering * Kappa Delta * Kappa Delta Rho * Language and Cultural Institute * Latin Link * Lee Hall * National Society of Collegiate Scholars * National Society of Minorities in Hospitality * New River Community College ESL * Newman Community * Pamplin LEAP * Panhellenic VT * PAX * Phi Sigma Pi * Physical Therapy Club * Pi Alpha Xi * Pre-Med without Borders * RU Women's Basketball * Residential Leadership Community * Rotaract * SERVE * Sigma Alpha Lambda * Sociological Association * Student African American Sisterhood * Student Athlete Advisory Committee * Student Council for Exceptional Children * Student Dietetic Association * Student Engineer Council * Student Teacher Interns * Sustainable Food Corps * Tau Beta Sigma * Undergraduate Biomedical Engineering Society * Universities Fighting World Hunger * Via Department of Civil and Environmental Engineering * VMRCVM-Graduate Student Association * VT Baseball Team * VT Men's Basketball * VT Softball Team * Corp of Cadets Bravo Company * Corp of Cadets Foxtrot Company * VT Engage * VT Men's Rugby Club * Zeta Tau Alpha
Corporate Partners	1901 Group * Anderson and Associates * ATK at the Radford Arsenal * Bank of America * BB&T Lighthouse Foundation * Cellar Restaurant * DISH Network * Feeding America* First Bank and Trust-Christiansburg * Food Lion-Hethwood * Highway 55 Restaurant * Institute for Critical Technology and Applied Science * JPI a

Type of Partnership	Partners
	HUBzone Co * In Balance Yoga Studio * Independent Velo * Kool Smiles Dental * Kroger on University City Blvd * Lisa Acciai, Graphic Designer * Long & Foster Realtors * MOOG Component Group * Moss in the New River Valley * New River Engraving * NRV Dental * NRV Macaroni Kids * NRVCS * NRV Realtor Association * Nest Realty * Polymer Solutions Inc * Pulaski County Chamber of Commerce * Rackspace * Rainbow Riders * Skanska Builders * Stage2Smile * StellarOne Christiansburg Service Center * Strange Coffee Co * Suntrust Bank-Christiansburg * Sylvan Learning Centers * Three Birds Berry Farm * Wall Brothers Dairy Farm * Well Hung Vineyards
Grant Partners	Adobe Employee Community Foundation * Blacksburg Newcomer's Club * Blacksburg Presbyterian Church Endowment * Community Foundation of the New River Valley * Evangelical Lutheran Church in America Domestic Hunger * Food Lion Charitable Foundation * Kroger Foundation * One Love Foundation * Private Foundations * Sodexo * Thrivent Financial for Lutherans * Vanguard Charitable Endowment Program * Virginia Interfaith Center for Public Policy * Walmart Foundation * YSA.org
Interfaith Partners	Alleghany Baptist Church * Belmont Christian Church * Blacksburg Baptist Church * Blacksburg Baptist Church Youth Group * Blacksburg Christian Church * Blacksburg Christian Fellowship * Blacksburg First Wesleyan * * Blacksburg Jewish Community Center * Blacksburg Jewish Community Center Sunday School Classes * Blacksburg Presbyterian Church * Blacksburg Presbyterian Church Endowment * Blacksburg United Methodist Church (BUMC) * Blacksburg United Methodist Church Women * Blacksburg Young Life * Christ Episcopal Church * Glade Church * Grace Covenant Presbyterian Church * GraceLife Church Youth Group * Grove United Methodist Church * LDS Single Adult Ward * LDS Youth Group * Luther Memorial Lutheran Church * Lutheran Men in Mission * The Lutheran Student Movement at VT * Lydia & Ruth Circles at BUMC * MMMM at Blacksburg United Methodist Church

Type of Partnership	Partners
	* New Life Christian Fellowship * New Mt. Zion Lutheran Church * Northside Presbyterian Church * Northstar * Park United Methodist Church * Price's Fork United Methodist Church * Shiloh Lutheran Church * St. Mary's Catholic Church * St Mary's Youth Group * St. Michael Lutheran Church * Unitarian Universalist Church of the NRV * Virginia Synod (ELCA) * Virginia Feeds Kids

Micah's Caring Initiative benefits from the work of outstanding student interns obtained through academic programs and units at Virginia Tech—for example, from classes that require students to engage in volunteer work. In addition, we participate in Virginia Tech's work-study program where students work with us to help pay for their education, with funding from the U.S. government. Students who become interns or have work-study positions with us gain valuable experiences that serve them well in the job market. They also gain greater understanding of community needs, program development and implementation, and the complexities of hunger. As Sarah Brooks one Virginia Tech student recalls,

> When first volunteering, I never absorbed how exorbitant the number of bags we packed were. It wasn't until I started interning that I fully grasped that it isn't just a number. Behind the 266 bags are 266 children who worry about where their next meal will come from or who may have very little, if anything to eat on the weekends when school is not in session.

Several departments at the university have hosted food drives for Micah's Backpack. We have also collected unused food items from students moving out of the dorms. At the conclusion of one spring semester, we salvaged 5,412 food items, eliminating food waste, engaging students with the Blacksburg community, and helping us stock up for the summer mobile backpack program. All of these efforts have helped raise awareness about hunger in the community and provided students and community members opportunities to help make a difference.

Students in Virginia Tech's business school have had assignments that require them to create entrepreneurial projects to benefit local nonprofits. One semester for example, students spent a day operating a lemonade stand outside of a grocery store to support the Initiative. In addition to purchasing drinks, many customers donated change to increase the students' profit. Not only did the students create and operate a one-and-done small business, they shared the story of childhood hunger in our community in a new way with a wide audience.

Students sometimes discover new ways to impact our outreach processes and products that I've never considered. For example, engineering students reorganized our food storage room shelving for optimal workflow. Another student created a video of Thursday night food packing that we use as a primer for new volunteers and for internet inquiries about our program: https://www.youtube.com/watch?v=JyD9qjMghUw

Connections to Virginia Tech have also helped us financially. Recently we were accepted into the Commonwealth of Virginia Campaign, a mechanism that enables state employees at Virginia Tech and other locations to make payroll deductions to nonprofit organizations. The first year, the Initiative received around $6,000 through the campaign, ranking eleventh among the hundreds of participating charities. We expect this donation to rise as Micah's Caring Initiative becomes even better known. Inclusion in the campaign represents deepened engagement with Virginia Tech and an important large-scale opportunity for program exposure, impact, sustainability, and growth.

Virginia Tech's student athletes help Micah's Backpack by conducting food drives, providing volunteers, and advocating for the program through social media. For example, the women's soccer team hosted a food drive at a women's lacrosse game with the Sports Promotion Department, players, and the Student-Athlete Advisory Committee tweeting about the event. The drive resulted in donations of more than three hundred granola bars. According to athletic adviser Natalie Forbes, "I definitely think that Micah's Backpack recognizes the values that Virginia Tech Athletics, and our university as a whole has to offer. . . This organization gives our athletes a chance to serve the community and really see the difference that they can make." At various times, the men's baseball and basketball team, among others, have helped to pack weekend bags of food at St. Michael for Micah's Backpack.

Through our relationship with a variety of partners we continue to discover important lessons to help the Caring Initiative grow and prosper. For example, our partnership with Virginia Tech students, faculty, and staff have made very visible the importance of aligning missions between the two organizations and the joint belief that effective community development on and off campus is a mutual effort. We also experienced the importance of critical events created by the university to help us expand and deepen our impact - acceptance into the Commonwealth of Virginia Campaign and the attention of Virginia Tech Athletics.

Our work with Virginia Tech has helped us fully develop the practice of providing multiple ways for people to engage in understanding and alleviating hunger in our community. We realize that the transient nature of a university community requires many short term and diverse ways to participate in community change. Respecting differences in the ways students wish to engage with the Initiative has helped us learn about and adopt new innovations, greatly expand our resources, and amplify our presence, purpose, and impact. Our relationship with Virginia Tech reveals just a fraction of the benefits we've received through reciprocal partnerships with many entities across our community.

CHAPTER 8
Developing

Volunteers Are Unique Partners and Leaders

The Micah's Caring Initiative programs meet volunteers where they are and encourage them to share their enthusiasm for helping others to make our community a better place. We always try to recognize the talent and skills that each person brings to the work. Letting volunteers participate as they'd like represents an important way that we acknowledge what people have to offer. We believe everyone contributes in his or her own way and in their own time. When we empower people to share their talents, we build a stronger program. Having a stronger program, in turn, helps increase participation, raises awareness about the issues we address, and strengthens our sustainability. This collaborative yet tailored approach to community engagement means we can have more short- and long-term impact with our outreach.

For example, more extroverted volunteers often oversee crowd control at the beginning of the food packing line, asking trivia questions and telling jokes to keep people entertained. At the other end of the line, sorting bags by schools is the province of people who like to organize. And the most physically energetic and robust volunteers tend to clean up and load volunteer vehicles for delivery. For the most part, people self-select activities to participate in, but when a particular task arises, organizers who are familiar with the volunteers try to select someone whose skills match the job.

Giving people the freedom to do what they like has many benefits including developing leadership skills. One student intern, loved working with MBP because I felt that my skills were recognized and valued. Jennie always gave me constructive comments and told me ways that she appreciated the work I did. I always felt great about myself and the job I was doing when I had to turn in evaluations for my field study because Jennie wrote down such positive things about me.

By recognizing the skills that she had to offer and allowing her to grow as a community builder, we helped her become a leader. Another student intern echoes these sentiments,

As a student working towards a Business Leadership minor, I am thankful that Micah's Backpack has given me the opportunity to really develop my leadership skills and get experience working with others. On a couple of Thursdays, I had the chance to lead MBP with Jasmine, another student intern, when Jennie was unable to be present. I was able to train and interact with volunteers and share our story about MBP. Doing so has allowed me to be more comfortable with public speaking, which was actually a weakness of mine before coming into this job. I have found that my role with MBP has granted me endless opportunities to better myself as a person and a leader.

Shaun Riebl, a graduate teaching assistant, agrees, "Anything the students did was recognized and each student always felt valued after volunteering at MBP. Jennie and other MBP 'regulars' or leaders would always recognize people and voice appreciation for the variety of ways someone can help."

When volunteers engage in enjoyable ways, they feel a sense of pride, joy, and personal growth in their work. That feeling, in turn, makes them valuable stakeholders in the process and the program. According to longtime volunteer Stacie Castro, "It has been so much fun to watch and see how MBP has grown over the years because of using different individuals' different skills and strengths. [I] cannot wait to see how it continues to move forward."

My efforts at hospitality succeed when I learn something about a volunteer that helps me connect them to a part of the packing night they especially enjoy or to another part of the Micah's Caring Initiative. For example, once I learned a high school volunteer was a math whiz I put him in charge of periodically conducting a physical inventory of supplies. He loves participating in this way because he gets to stretch his math muscles. Or when a volunteer mentions in passing that she recently purchased shoes for her grandchildren then it's a natural part of the conversation to bring up Micah's Closet and then gauge her interest and possibly encouraging her to assist with that program.

Student interns seem to really appreciate this personalized approach. Typically over the course of a semester as they experience packing nights, their natural strengths are revealed. For example, interns have different talents and I encourage them to develop in the areas that appeal most to them. One intern does an exceptional job welcoming volunteers and explaining the packing night process to new folks. I send new volunteers to her as we prepare to pack because she has a wonderful way of making them feel welcome and appreciated. I imagine this skill will help her in her future employment in the human development field. The climate we promote in the Micah's programs helps connect volunteers to the types of outreach that appeal to them.

Our work with and developing volunteers has revealed important considerations and practices for success. We are volunteer-centered because we realize that the more satisfied a volunteer is, the more hours they will commit. Satisfied volunteers also market the program positively and in new ways. They often bring friends and neighbors into the Initiative to enjoy working together.

We realize that volunteers bring important resources to the success of our program. These include economic resources, experiences, skills, time, connections and lived community culture - history, traditions, and norms. We've discovered that volunteer motivation to participate comes from a variety of reasons. People volunteer because it will help their career, they are altruistic and simply want to help others, they have personal beliefs that support volunteering, they want a socially just or healthier community, they are lonely and want to fight isolation, they want to learn, or volunteering makes them feel better or helps them work through challenging personal situations. Sometimes volunteers simply want to give back to the community or the organization that has helped them. In some instances, our volunteers have had critical or spiritual events in their life that lead them to assisting with our Caring Initiative.

Even though volunteers are motivated to join us for specific reasons, they often grow and develop in unintentional ways. Students who simply intend to complete service hours or a work-study job also gain enhanced self-esteem, leadership skills, and an ethic of service. Volunteers who are fighting isolation often develop new perspectives about the people they are serving with. Some volunteers who have a deep volunteer ethic sometimes find they become attracted to promoting social justice in the community. Most importantly, volunteers with our programs tend to improve their health and wellbeing while they do the same for those they serve.

The volunteers who make the Initiative successful have a variety of volunteer motivations and resources and they are also a diverse group of people. Our volunteers cross gender, race, education, economic, geographical, and age categories. They also bring a wide variety of perspectives about the community, life, and volunteering to our efforts.

Creating an environment that respects, supports, and develops this diverse community of volunteers takes a lot of time and requires strong intentionality. It can be difficult to be volunteer-centered and at the same time not compromise the principles or brand of the Caring Initiative. Program coordinators plan, implement, and assess the best ways to identify, select, orient, train, use, recognize, and evaluate each volunteer.

In addition to implementing good volunteer development, program coordinators create a transformational space to help volunteers grow and learn together while effectively and efficiently accomplishing the work of the program. We've found creating this space requires a strong partnership between the coordinator or lead volunteers and other volunteers. There also needs to be an opportunity for volunteers to think critically about their personal assumptions behind their work and their world. Sometimes program leaders use a critical event such as a program disappointment, unexpected success, or a personal dilemma to help spur change. Transformation of perspectives and practices is also enhanced through the differing personal characteristics of the volunteers including their personality, work styles, and worldviews that stretch and challenge those around them to see things in new ways.

Most importantly we've tried to be architects of a caring and enjoyable volunteer environment by supporting individual independence and interdependence with others. We know that individuals, families, and groups excel when they retain their own autonomy while engaging in joint action. Through our own unique growth and development as volunteers, we find many ways to help our neighbors alleviate hunger and live better lives.

CHAPTER 9
Doing and Expanding

Starting Your Own Caring Initiative

Hungry students and families all over the United States could benefit from backpack feeding programs. These programs are a wonderful way for an interfaith or community group to make a difference in their community. We hope that the information we share based on some of the lessons we have learned over nearly a decade, will help other groups get started. Check out our website at: www.micahsbackpack.org.

Micah's Backpack began with a few passionate people, a partner school, and a funding source. At our initial interest meeting, we gathered six people to discuss the possibility of starting a program. From that meeting, we established our school partner, who would be responsible for buying the food, packing, and delivering the backpacks. We each took on tasks since there was no specific coordinator. We also determined how many backpacks we thought we could afford to deliver through the end of the school year.

We advise groups to start small with your current strengths and interests and then build up to meet the need. Starting small gives you the opportunity to work out details and make sure you have solid financial and volunteer support in place before you commit to a large number of participants. A small group allows people to get to know each other making it easier to keep track of the details and to get clear on the program principles and procedures.

We started with grant money from Thrivent Financial for Lutherans and then asked individuals, interfaith groups, and civic organizations to sponsor backpacks for a weekend, semester, or year. We found people happy to contribute to a program that made a direct, positive impact on the lives of children. Additionally, we have found that equipping our volunteers to be program ambassadors is a helpful way to build sustainability of resources. When the people most dedicated to your program have the power to spread the word then good things tend to happen. For example with more volunteers and more community buy-in, then additional funding will appear.

It is extremely helpful to partner with a nonprofit group such as a church that can handle donations, tax receipts, and attract and manage grant funding. If that is not possible, designation of 501c3 nonprofit status from the Internal Revenue Service is needed so people can deduct their donations to the program when they file their income tax returns. We have found that having one overarching institution anchor the initiative also facilitates risk taking, growth, and community engagement especially when the leadership of the organization believes in these approaches. This type of leadership helps the Initiative stay focused on the common goal, assists with managing growth of programs, and helps keep the Initiative vibrant to prevent decline.

We initially used actual backpacks for distributing food, and soon switched to doubled plastic grocery bags. Our partner schools place these bags in the students' backpacks. This change has streamlined the program and works well for us and our partners. It also allows us to put funding into the food rather than the packaging of the food. Our packing process includes each volunteer carrying a bag along a circuit, picking up food items on a series of tables as they walk the circuit. Photos of this packing system are found on our website: www.micahsbackpack.org and this video: https://www.youtube.com/watch?v=ldGn8lBrlvs.

At first, we purchased all food from a local grocery store and asked for donations of specific items from individuals and groups. Now we obtain food from multiple sources, including the grocery store where we buy by the case and receive discounts, a warehouse store, a food distributer, and our local food bank. In addition, various community groups conduct food drives on our behalf. From our perspective, most helpful are "clean" food drives, held at a local grocery store. Entering customers are offered a list of items to purchase. When they leave the store, customers give the food directly to the volunteers running the drive. We consider this food clean mainly because there's no question about how or where it was stored or for how long. Food drives may also be held during club/group meetings or sporting events or by collecting food from a neighborhood. We currently spend between four and six dollars per student bag.

Each bag contains fifteen food items and an educational piece. We seem to provide a little more food than similar feeding programs. Our goal is to send home the most nutritional, shelf-stable, and easy-to-prepare food available. We rotate items to offer variety. Student interns have developed our educational pieces, which provide fun activities such as word searches and information on healthy eating.

As a best practice, we send timely thank you notes as we develop relationships with individuals and donor groups. We supplement the thank yous with monthly email reports describing the program's accomplishments through data and photographs. We determined our indicators of success early in the program so we would have intentional and consistent reporting over the years (i.e. number of meals, number of students, etc.).

We feel strongly that thank you notes should not be accompanied by requests for additional funding. Asking for a donation at the time of the thank you diminishes the value of the thank you. A thank you letter shouldn't multi-task. Funding plays an important role in the success of the program and should be requested under separate cover. We also send semiannual thank you letters to the school staff who facilitate bag distribution, to delivery volunteers, and to individuals or groups who hold food drives.

For us, building a partnership with community groups and businesses has been key to the success of the Initiative. We have about 250 community partners who work with Micah's Backpack and a fluid team of people who pack each Thursday night for about an hour, including numerous students from Virginia Tech. The university student engagement office and nutrition or human development departments have been helpful partners for engaging students. Many campus groups appreciate volunteer opportunities and happily get involved in a program that provides food for our community's low-resource youth.

We encourage volunteering in our work for a wide variety of individuals, the young and young at heart, and academic, civic, collegiate, and interfaith groups. We don't take attendance or require a commitment—people can come once, every week, or whenever they feel like it. We try to create a culture that allows them to contribute in a way that meets their needs as well as the needs of our program by offering small every day opportunities for people to participate in our work.

Most of all, we've learned that success breeds success. Micah's Backpack program developed strong partnerships at the individual, organization, and community levels and served as a model that enabled additional programs to quickly gain traction. The spin-off programs have filled niches of need not only for low-resource families but also for volunteers. This means we've had to strategically manage our growth by staying clearly focused on our common goal and operating principles.

Most important to the success of a caring initiative is the quality of the coordinators of the programs. Our coordinators believe in collaborative leadership that empowers others to improve, learn, be accountable, and take ownership of issues through an ethic of caring. Coordinators have consistent and clear processes for handling conflict and making program decisions. They are also well aware of the internal and external factors impacting or potentially impacting their program. They tend to be selfless social innovators in their service to the participants, volunteers, and partners they serve. These coordinators encourage unintended but important program outcomes by being flexible, supporting new ways of working and being, creating a culture of innovation, and encouraging ripple effects of the program. To ensure sustainability of the program they also work closely with the leadership of the host organization on a succession plan to prepare for a time when their work as a coordinator concludes. The coordinator is key to community change.

CHAPTER 10
Wrapping Up

Final Thoughts

When we started Micah's Backpack and the subsequent outreach programs of Micah's Caring Initiative there wasn't a *how-to manual*. We just decided we would do our best to try to improve the lives of others: participants, volunteers, and partners. When we have kept that goal as our focus, we have found ways to help people from low-resource households improve their quality of life. When doing this, we are also helping everyone. The community believes in our mission, and that support has allowed us to expand the program, build a better community, and experience unexpected benefits.

I'm grateful to have had the opportunity to share the Micah's Backpack story of making a difference. I've been able to use my skills as a writer to share information, raise money, and advocate for caring for our neighbors. Likewise, my natural tendency toward hospitality has helped make the Micah's Backpack experience a specific environment for volunteers. Understanding the value of what others have to offer did not come naturally for me, I learned it over time. Without a doubt it is one of my greatest personal outcomes. We've shared our best practices with others interested in helping people. From down the highway to across the country, communities have created backpack programs after connecting with us. We've had opportunities to help build something bigger than ourselves and

I value that experience. Courtney Grohs, the president of the board of our local community foundation, writes,

> The Community Foundation of the New River Valley has supported many weekend feeding programs in our area, but Micah's Backpack has always stood out as an exemplary program. The board and staff have been impressed with the deliberate and sensitive way in which Micah's Backpack goes about its work, trying new things and constantly looking for ways to make the children served feel special.

If you're reading this and wondering "Can I do it?" I say emphatically, "Trust your instincts. Follow your dreams. Go out and make a difference!"

ABOUT THE AUTHORS

Jennie Hodge recalls stories her father told her of mayonnaise sandwiches and going hungry. Those stories and others led her to advocate for children's food programs. In 2011, she became the director of Micah's Backpack, a weekend food program for low-resource children. In 2012, Hodge started Micah's Garden, a community garden co-op. She went on to create Micah's Mobile Backpack, which broadened the scope of the food program. She lives with her family in Summerfield, North Carolina.

Nancy Franz loves nurturing community, organizational, and leadership development. She worked for 33 years with the Cooperative Extension System as a faculty member and administrator in adult and youth development. She enjoys volunteering, outdoor pursuits, gardening, reading, and consuming dark chocolate. She lives with her husband in Ames, Iowa.

WORKS CITED

Arkansas Rice Depot. *Food for Kids Provides Hungry Children in Arkansas with Backpacks Filled with Kid Friendly Food*, http://ricede.brinkster.net/ffk.asp .

Beere, Carole, James Votruba, and Gail Wells. *Becoming an Engaged Campus: A Practical Guide for Instutuionalizing Public Engagement*. San Francisco: CA, John Wiley & Sons, Inc., 2011.

Blacksburg Estates Ministries. *Blacksburg United Methodist Church Blacksburg Estates Ministries Comments*. http://www.blacksburgumc.org/#!fun143/cg9p

Bielefeld, Wolfgang, and William Suhs Cleveland. "Faith-based Organizations as Service Providers and their Relationship to Government." *Nonprofit and Voluntary Sector Quarterly*, 2013, Volume 42, Number 3.

Butler Flora, Cornelia and Jan Flora. *Rural Communities: Legacy and Change*. Boulder, CO: Westview Press, 2012.

Callahan, Kennon. *The Twelve Keys Leaders' Guide: An Approach for Grassroots, Key Leaders, and Pastors Together*. San Francisco, CA: Jossey-Bass, 2010.

Christensen, Clayton. *The Innovator's Dilemma*. Boston, MA: Harvard Business School Press, 1997.

CLRSearch.com – We Know Real Estate Search. *CLRSearch*. http://www.claytonchristensen.com/books/the-innovators-dilemma/

Clinical and Translations Science Awards Consortium Community Engagement Key Function Committee Task Force on the Principles of Community Engagement. *Principles of Community Engagement*, Washington, D.C., National Institutes of Health, 2011.

Community Foundation of the New River Valley. *Micah's Backpack Goes Mobile with Community Impact Grant*. https://cfnrv.org/images/page/CIGP_Micahs_Backpack1.pdf

Crabtree, Russell. *Owl Sight: Evidence-Based Discernment and the Promise of Organizational Intelligence for Ministry*. Columbus, OH: Magi Press, 2012.

Feeding America Southwest Virginia. *Mobile Food Pantry to Help Serve Those in Need*.

Feldstein, Lew. *Social Capital: Better Together*. Concord, NH: New Hampshire Charitable Foundation, 2002.

Food and Nutrition Service. *Summer Food Service Program SFSP. http://www.fns.usda. gov/sfsp/summer-food-service-program* .

Franz, Nancy. "Second Generation Volunteer Administration: Moving from Transaction to Transformative Volunteer Learning Environments." *International Journal of Volunteer Administration*, 2008, Volume 25, Number 2.

Franz, Nancy, Barry Garst, Sarah Baughman, Chris Smith, and Brian Peters. Catalyzing Transformation: Conditions in Extension Educational Environments that Promote Change. *Journal of Extension, Volume 47, Number 4*, 2009.

Gladwell, Malcolm. *The Tipping Point*. New York: Little, Brown and Company, 2002.

Gray, Barbara. *Collaborating: Finding Common Ground for Multiparty Problems*, San Francisco: CA, Jossey-Bass, 1989.

Heath, Chip, and Dan Heath. *Made to Stick: Why Some Ideas Survive and Others Die*. New York: Random House, 2008.

Hodge, Jennie. Micah's Mobile Backpack: An Evolution in Alleviating Weekend Food Insecurity. http://foodstudies.cgpublisher.com/product/pub.292/prod.2

Hunger Doesn't Take a Vacation. http://frac.org/pdf/summer_report_2011.pdf

Kretzmann, John, and John McKnight. *Building Communities from the Inside Out: A Path Toward Finding and Mobilizing a Community's Assets*. Chicago, IL: ACTA Publications, 1993.

Micah's Caring Initiative. www.st-michael-lutheran-church.org/ministries/micahs-caring-initiative

Morse, Suzanne. *Smart Communities: How Citizens and Local Leaders Can Use Strategic Thinking to Build a Brighter Future.* San Francisco, CA: Jossey-Bass, 2004.

Nodding, Nel. Caring: A Feminine Approach to Ethics and Moral Education. Berkely, CA: University of California Press, 1984.

Schneider, Jo Anne, and Patricia Wittberg. "Comparing Practical Theology Across Religions and Denominations." *Journal of the Religious Research Association,* Volume 52, 2011.

Senge, Peter. *The Fifth Discipline: The Art & Practice of The Learning Organization.* New York, Doubleday, 1990.

Virginia Department of Education. *Program Statistics & Reports.* http://www.doe.virginia.gov/statistics_reports/

CPSIA information can be obtained at www.ICGtesting.com
Printed in the USA
LVIW01n1457141216
517258LV00010B/94